One-Sentence Reader Reviews for *No More No*

"No More No is like a breath of fresh love…."

"A must read for every believer."

"The stories shared in *No More No* open your eyes to see how a loving word spoken can change a life."

"I was encouraged to know that I am not alone in many of the struggles I've had learning to trust God and hear His voice."

"A wonderfully written book…for those honestly pressing in and wanting to hear God and recognize those promptings."

"I've always been shy, but now I have the courage to walk up to someone when the Lord tells me to pray for them."

"Reading Julie's book stirred the embers of a desire I've always had—to share the good news that God loves people and is for them, not against them."

"I loved the combination of the testimonies, the Word of God and personal stories."

"Jesus kept the gospel simple and profound, and I believe Julie Earl has done the same in *No More No*."

"If you need help to get over the fear of stepping out, this book is for you!"

"Julie makes it so easy and practical."

"I finished my book and can't wait to read it again…such a faith builder."

"I believe that everyone who reads this book will be encouraged to say 'yes' to God's promptings."

"We highly recommend the *No More No* book and Study Guide to be a leadership and personal evangelism tool for the Body of Christ."

STUDY GUIDE

No More No

SAY YES TO GOD AND LET HIM SPEAK, WORK AND LOVE THROUGH YOU

JULIE EARL

♥CAYM
Publishing

McKinney, Texas

Library of Congress Control Number: 2017919187

ISBN: 978-0-9861033-3-9

Pronouns referring to God have been capitalized out of respect and honor.
Cover concept by Julie Earl
Cover art and layout by Eric Nishimoto and Shig Katada
Photography by Shig Katada—www.KatadaKreations.com

Visit Julie Earl at: www.CrazyAboutYou.org

Julie's Thanks:
A heartfelt and incredibly huge thank you to Lois Harker and Janice Spurgin for your help with editing, and to Nicole Williamson for your help with formatting. You ladies are amazing and a gift from Jesus.

Thank you to Shig Katada for once again sweetly working with me to create the cover. You are such a servant of Jesus.

A special thanks to the awesome beta test Bible study group in Marion, Ohio who did this study as I was writing it. I so appreciated your ideas.

Thank you again to my Jesus and my family. You are my treasure!

Table of Contents

Greetings from Julie

Whether you are doing this study on your own or in a group, I'm excited you have joined me on this journey of discovering that God wants to speak, work and love through you wherever you go. You get to throw away formulas, forget your fears and let God flow through you as you tune into what He wants to say and do!

Directions:

Two Versions: Each week you have the option to choose the "Quick Version" or the "Going Deeper Version" of this study:

- In the "Quick Version," you will only do the reading from *No More No* and participate in the "You Can Do It" weekly activities.

- In the "Going Deeper Version," the reading, questions and teachings are broken up into four short sections for you to do on four separate days or all at once each week — you choose.

- I worked hard to keep each section short since I know how busy we all are, so I would encourage you to try to do the "Going Deeper Version" each week to get all you can from this study.

Group Wrap-Up: If you are doing this study with a group, the group leader(s) will read the discussion questions in the "Group Wrap-Up" out loud each week to discuss the previous week's content. [Leaders, make sure to read the Leader's Guide and Tips in the back of the book.] If you are doing this study alone, the "Group Wrap-Up" is a great opportunity for review. (Just skip the parts that apply only to a group.)

Practice in a Safe Place and **You Can Do It:** (These hands-on activities are life changing, so if you aren't in a group find people to practice with.)

Practice in a Safe Place gives you the chance to practice hearing God's voice as He speaks to your thoughts for others. Start simple and don't stress. Cheer for each other when you hear incorrectly because that means you were willing to take risks. Remember, every believer can hear God's voice once they silence the lies of the enemy that say they can't!

You Can Do It gives you the chance to express God's love and power in a world where people desperately need to know God sees them and loves them. You will do certain exercises every week as you are at work, school, the store or the coffee shop—and your fears will diminish as your love grows. (Don't worry, I start out easy!)

Group Outreaches: Your group will do 2 or 3 low-stress outreaches to simply love people (one during class time at the Week 6 Group Wrap-Up meeting and one or two outside of class time on another day of the week). Remember, when you do the outreaches feel free to just watch until you are comfortable saying something.

A Typical Outreach (usually 2 to 2½ hours) might look like this:
- (30 min.) Meet at someone's home or at a restaurant.
    - Share an inspirational word and scriptures.
    - Pray together to break off lies and doubts of the enemy.
- (60-90 min.) Get in groups of 2 and go to area stores, parks or neighborhoods as the Holy Spirit leads. (Or go in groups of 4 and break up into groups of 2 once you are there.)
- You might:
    - Tell someone God highlighted them with His love and express God's words of love for them.
    - Tell someone that you are praying God's blessings for people and ask if they have any prayer needs. (Then pray with them.)
    - Ask God to give you a word for someone and then express that word along with other things God tells you.
    - Pray for someone who you sense has health issues or you can see has health issues. Then have them test it out.
- (30 min.) Get back together as a group to share stories and pray.

NOTE: There are Conversation Starters on pp. 145-146 in the back of this guide. If you have questions, contact us at www.CrazyAboutYou.org.

Kickoff Meeting

Group Session #1: [Everything not in brackets can be read out loud to the group by the leader. Directions meant for the leader are in brackets.]

- [Leaders, hand out *No More No* and the *No More No Bible Study Guide.* Don't forget to collect the money for the books.]

- Let's discuss the best options for communicating. [Gather contact information such as emails and phone numbers.]

- Can someone please open us in prayer?

- Everyone please share your name, occupation and family status (tell us if you are married, single, have children, etc.).

- I need someone to read "Why Read No More No" in *No More No* on p. 1.

- Will someone please read "In My Socks" from *No More No* on pp. 7-9?
    - ❖ What was the simple message God had for Matthew?
    - ❖ Has God prompted you to say or do something, and did you?

- I will read "Greetings from Julie" from this study guide on pp 7-8, discussing any questions you have as I read. [Read it to the group.]

- Now let's turn to "Week 1: God's Talking" on p. 13 of this study and look closely at the first week to make sure you understand what you will be doing each week on your own at home. [Discuss how it works.]

- Let's watch Julie's video entitled "Why the *No More No* Study Can Change Your Life and Your World" at www.CrazyAboutYou.org.

- Discuss:
    - ❖ What excites you about this study?
    - ❖ What are the most difficult struggles and fears you have when it comes to talking about Jesus?
    - ❖ Why do you suppose the demonic realm works so hard to stop you from expressing God's heart to your world?
- If you are comfortable, let's take turns praying short prayers of surrender to Jesus, asking Him to silence every lie and break every fear.

Prayer: [Leader continues to read out loud.]

There is a difference between saying pat prayers for your Uncle Joe's best friend's little sister's dog, and really learning how to minister to one another.

Let's make these weekly prayer times together not about our prayer lists, but about strengthening, encouraging and ministering to one another as the Holy Spirit directs our prayers.

Practice in a Safe Place:

[Leader asks]: If you are in need of personal ministry for something heavy on your heart, please raise your hand.

[Depending on the size of the group and the amount of time left, pick your option]:
    A. Have the whole group pray and minister to one person at a time. (Set them in a "hot seat" and gently place your hands on their shoulders, if appropriate, as you pray and hear from God for them.)
    B. Break up into smaller groups and do the same thing for those who need ministry.

Week 1:

God's Talking

Week 1: God's Talking
Quick Version

Prayer:

Thank you, Father, for sending your Spirit, the Holy Spirit, to speak to me, lead me and empower me to do everything Jesus did. I want to receive all you have for me so that I can be your hands, your voice and your feet on the earth.

You Can Do It:

Pray silently for everyone you pass or interact with all week.

As you pass people at work, school, in stores and while you're driving or walking, ask God to bless them, open their eyes to His truth, soften their hearts to His love, free them from lies of the devil or whatever you feel prompted to pray. You'll be amazed how your love for people will grow!

Read:

No More No pp. 7-21 (Chapter 1—God's Talking)

Reading time: 19 minutes

Notes, comments or questions from your reading, and ideas for applying it to your life:

Week 1: God's Talking
Going Deeper

Prayer:

Thank you, Father, for sending your Spirit, the Holy Spirit, to speak to me, lead me and empower me to do everything Jesus did. I want to receive all you have for me so that I can be your hands, your voice and your feet on the earth.

You Can Do It:

Pray silently for everyone you pass or interact with all week.

As you pass people at work, school, in stores and while you're driving or walking, ask God to bless them, open their eyes to His truth, soften their hearts to His love, free them from lies of the devil or whatever you feel prompted to pray. You'll be amazed how your love for people will grow!

Section 1—Born Again

Read: (In your reading you will typically stop and start at the subtitles on the pages listed.)

No More No pp. 9-11 (Chapter 1—God's Talking)

Verse: (Pray it as you say it 5 times.)

"No one can see the kingdom of God unless he is born again."
John 3:3b

1. My mother was taught that you had to go to church and be good enough in order to please God and earn your right to go to heaven. What were you taught and what do you believe now?

2. Read John 3:1-8. What did Jesus say was required to go to heaven and see the kingdom of God?

3. In verses 4-8 Jesus explains what it means to be born again. When we are born through our mother's womb, we are born of water—*"flesh gives birth to flesh"* (verse 6), but when we are "born again" God's Spirit gives new life to our spirits—*"the Spirit gives birth to spirit."* If you have been born again, what changes did you experience when God's Spirit gave new life to your spirit? If you have not yet been born again, have you seen changes in others who have had this experience?

4. Second Corinthians 5:17 says, *"...if anyone is in Christ, he is a new creation; the old has gone, the new has come!"* Verse 21 says that you become *"the righteousness of God."* When you believe that Jesus is who He says He is—the Son of God who came to take away the sins of the world—and when you turn from a life of doing your own thing and ask Him to be in charge (or Lord) of your life, you become a new person whom God sees as forgiven and holy. If you have not yet been made a new creation and been born again, would you like to be made new? Why?

5. Read John 3:16-18. You will receive forgiveness and eternal life by simply believing in Jesus and making Him the driver (Lord) of your life. If you still struggle to believe in Jesus or you don't know enough about Jesus, then begin reading the sections of the Bible that talk about Jesus' life on the earth. Matthew, Mark, Luke and John all talk about Jesus' life. Matthew is a great place to start!

Response:

If you are ready to believe in Jesus as your Savior and you want Him to be the "driver" in your life, then read pages 223-226 in *No More No* (where I explain more in-depth how to become born again). God is passionately in love with you and yearns for you to receive the forgiveness, intimacy and guidance that were provided when Jesus died for your sins on the cross.

Jesus spoke to my heart one day and said that while He was hanging on the cross He saw me and loved me—and He saw you and loved you too!

Section 2—Baptized (Filled) with the Holy Spirit

Read:

No More No pp. 11-16 (Chapter 1—God's Talking)

Verse: (Pray it as you say it 5 times.)

"If you then, though you are evil, know how to give good gifts to your children, how much more will your Father in heaven give the Holy Spirit to those who ask him!"

Luke 11:13

1. Insights from this verse:

2. When you become born again, God's Spirit gives you a new spirit that is righteous and holy in His sight. Because your sins are no longer held against you, God's Spirit is able to come and live inside you. As a born-again believer, you have the opportunity to not only be a child of God but to receive the baptism of the Holy Spirit. Some receive this baptism when they are saved and some receive it at a later time once they learn this gift is available. That part is a bit of a mystery, but the bottom line is that we can simply ask God to give us all He has for us—and trust that He will!

   If you have received the baptism of the Holy Spirit, when did it take place and what is your story? If you are not sure you have received the baptism of the Holy Spirit, what are your questions?

3. Read Acts 1:4-8. In verse 4 Jesus told the disciples to wait for (expect to receive) the gift of the Holy Spirit. We, too, have to expect to receive the Holy Spirit. Notice in Acts chapter 2 that all the other God-fearing Jews who were in Jerusalem didn't receive the gift of the Holy

16

Spirit because they didn't have an expectation to receive. Some of them even mocked those who received. This shows us that the Holy Spirit doesn't force Himself on people. We have to expect and receive Him—and His gifts—by faith.

4. In Acts 1:5 Jesus said that John baptized (immersed) in water, but they would be baptized (immersed) in the Holy Spirit. In verse 8 Jesus tells us the result of that baptism. Explain in your own words what happens when a believer is baptized in the Holy Spirit:

5. Read Acts 2 and see what happened when the Holy Spirit came. The Holy Spirit living within us changes everything! What stands out to you in Acts chapter 2?

6. Read Acts 2:38-39. These verses are helpful if you have been taught that the Holy Spirit and His gifts are no longer for believers.

   According to these verses, who is the promise of the Holy Spirit for (and consequently His gifts)?

Response:

Jesus said to come to Him as a child—with faith and simplicity—so if you are willing and have not yet done so, ask God to immerse and baptize you in His Spirit. Then trust Him, as a beloved child trusts a beloved Father, to give you what you ask for—the Holy Spirit in His fullness!

Write your experience in a journal (whether you notice any changes yet or not) and tell several people that you have invited the Holy Spirit to immerse you in Himself and to lead you moment by moment.

Section 3—Why the Devil Hates the Gift of Tongues

Read:

No More No pp. 14-16 [Re-read if needed] (Chapter 1—God's Talking)

Verse: (Pray it as you say it 5 times.)

"I thank God that I speak in tongues more than all of you."

1 Corinthians 14:18

1. How much did Paul pray in tongues and why do you think he did? Was it a good gift? Did it impact Paul's life?

2. I have a competition going with the apostle Paul to see if I can pray in tongues more than he did. I'm not sure if that *"great cloud of witnesses"* in heaven can see and hear us (see Hebrews 12:1), so if they can't I asked Jesus to let Paul know about the competition. Paul's passion for praying in tongues was an important key to the love, power and revelation he had. Would you like to follow Paul's example and join me in this competition? When we get to heaven, we can find out who won. (I'm pretty sure Jesus and Paul are chuckling with us about this!)

3. The Christians in Corinth must have been really enjoying the gift of tongues because Paul had to explain to them that praying in tongues in a group setting is only useful if it is interpreted. In doing so, he actually shared a number of incredible truths about the gift of tongues.

   Read where Paul talks about this in 1 Corinthians 14:1-18. I have broken down the truths on page 15 of *No More No*, but to help you remember them, write them in your own words:

4. Read pages 67-68 in *No More No* where I talk about the results of brain scans performed while people pray in tongues. What advantage can you see in quieting your mind so that your spirit can pray? Would your mind hinder or limit your understanding in ways that your born-again spirit would not?

5. Verse 16 says that when you pray in the Spirit you are praising God with your spirit. How neat that we are given another way to praise God! Psalm 22:3 (KJV) says, *"But thou art holy, O thou that inhabitest the praises of Israel."* If God inhabits our praises, that means when we praise Him while praying in tongues, He is able to draw nearer to us. As a result of His nearness, we have fullness of joy (Psalm 16:11).

   What are other benefits for God and for you when you spend time praising God as you pray in tongues? (Can you think of other verses?)

6. Why do you think the devil hates the gift of tongues and wants to keep you from enjoying all its blessings?

   What threat do you think praying in the Spirit (tongues) brings to the demonic world—to principalities and powers? (See Ephesians 6:12.)

Response:

Imagine offering your children an incredible gift and them being afraid to open it. Realizing your children don't trust you would hurt intensely. How much more it must hurt God's heart when we reject His gifts.

Ask God to silence the lies of the enemy about the gift of praying in another language, and by faith ask God to fill your mouth. Then begin speaking whatever non-English words come out. Trust God to pray and praise through your lips. You will be edified and your heart will bubble up with joy and love as His words flow through you.

Section 4—God Loves to Talk to Us and Through Us

Read:

No More No pp. 16-19 (Chapter 1—God's Talking)

Verse: (Pray it as you say it 5 times.)

"In the last days, God says, I will pour out my Spirit on all people. Your sons and daughters will prophesy"

Acts 2:17a

1. Since we are still in the last days until Jesus returns, you get to prophesy (share God's words with others) as His Spirit speaks to your thoughts. What an incredible gift!

    Read 1 Corinthians 14:3-4. What is the purpose of prophecy and why was Paul adamant that we eagerly desire and use this gift?

2. Some people misinterpret 1 Corinthians 13 and forget to read 1 Corinthians 14:1. Read these passages. Have prophecy, tongues and knowledge passed away?

    When does it say they will pass away? (See 1 Corinthians 13:8-12.)

    Even Paul, whose letters make up a large part of the New Testament, includes himself in the comment that *"for now we see through a glass, darkly"* (1 Cor. 13:12 KJV). Even with the great revelations Paul and other biblical writers had, none of us will know fully until we see God face to face in heaven. And how amazing that will be!

3. The devil constantly tells us we can't hear God's voice, but the Bible says when you become a new creature in Christ you are given the *"mind of Christ"* (1 Corinthians 2:16). Because you have the mind of Christ and are filled with the Holy Spirit, God is able to speak to you

20

and through you. God loves, loves, loves to talk *to* His children and *through* His children!

What lies has the enemy told you in regard to prophecy and your ability to hear God's voice?

What truths dispel those lies? (Hint: Do loving fathers talk to their children?)

4. In John 10:27 Jesus said, *"My sheep hear my voice."* What are several instances where you have heard God's voice and He strengthened, encouraged, comforted or guided you?

Response:

Take two minutes to listen for God's voice to your thoughts and write down His words of love for you:

Chapter Highlights: (*No More No* Pages 19-21)

Read the Chapter Highlights and Application for review and inspiration.

Week 1: Group Wrap-Up

Group Session #2

- [Discuss any business and collect payments still needed for books.]

- Will someone open us in prayer?

- Intro and last week's "You Can Do It":
    - ❖ Everyone tell your name and what happened as you silently prayed for people you passed or interacted with all week.
    - ❖ Did it impact you or change your attitude toward people?

- Next week's "You Can Do It":
    - ❖ Continue to pray for people silently and also chit-chat with strangers to let them know they are seen and important.
    - ❖ Write your "God Encounters" in the back of this study guide (pp. 137-144) or in a journal, or speak them into your voice recorder so that you don't forget them.
    - ❖ What are some opening comments and topics to chit-chat about with people wherever you go? (The weather, their shoes or outfit, their smile, their hard work, etc.)

Important Note for the Whole Group: Since there are numerous topics covered in the "Going Deeper" sections each week, the goal of the "Group Wrap-Up" is to bring out the most important points and to create an opportunity for discussion. The Wrap-Up doesn't follow along closely with the weekly work, so it may be easiest if you don't try to read along in your sections while the leader is reading the Wrap-Up questions. It may be easiest to simply read along in the Wrap-Up and just refer back to the sections when the leader directs you to do so.

- Section 1 Discussion: Born Again
    - ❖ Read John 3:3 and discuss what it means. [Always have various group members offer to read the passages out loud.]
    - ❖ Two people share in 1 or 2 minutes how you became born again and how it changed your life.
    - ❖ Read 2 Corinthians 5:17 and 5:21.
    - ❖ What does it mean to be a new creation and righteous?
    - ❖ Two people share in 1 or 2 minutes what areas changed in your life when you became a new creation and righteous.
    - ❖ Is there anyone who is investigating Jesus and Christianity? If so, do you have questions for the group?
    - ❖ Does anyone want to pray now or later to become born again?

- Section 2 Discussion: Baptized (Filled) with the Holy Spirit
  - ❖ Read Acts 1:3-5 and 1:8.
  - ❖ Why did Jesus send the Holy Spirit to baptize believers?
  - ❖ What are two important results of being baptized in the Holy Spirit (verse 8)?
  - ❖ Can two people share in 1 or 2 minutes what happened when you received the baptism of the Holy Spirit and what changes you have seen in your life as a result?
  - ❖ Read Acts 2:38-39.
  - ❖ Who is the promise of the Holy Spirit for?
  - ❖ Does anyone have questions?
  - ❖ Would anyone like to pray to receive the baptism of the Holy Spirit or to pray to be refreshed in the Holy Spirit? [Pray for this at the end of the meeting.]

- Section 3 Discussion: Why the Devil Hates the Gift of Tongues
  - ❖ Read Acts 2:1-4 and 11b-13.
  - ❖ How many were filled with the Holy Spirit and began to speak in tongues as the Spirit enabled them?
  - ❖ Does God want to empower and equip you to the same degree that He empowered and equipped the early church? Why?
  - ❖ Read what Paul said about tongues from page 15 of *No More No* or share the list that you wrote on p. 18 of this study guide (taken from 1 Corinthians 14:1-18).
  - ❖ If you pray in tongues, what benefits have you experienced?
  - ❖ Why do you think the devil hates this gift so much?
  - ❖ What questions do you have?
  - ❖ Would you like to allow God to pray through you in tongues since He knows exactly what you need? [Pray for this at the end of the meeting.]

- Section 4 Discussion: God Loves to Talk to Us and Through Us
  - ❖ Read 1 Corinthians 14:1-4.
  - ❖ What does it mean to prophesy?
  - ❖ What are the three main purposes of prophecy (verse 3)?
  - ❖ Read 1 Corinthians 13:8-12.
  - ❖ When will knowledge, tongues and prophecy disappear?
  - ❖ Read 1 Corinthians 2:16 and John 10:27.
  - ❖ If you have the mind of Christ and are one of His followers (His sheep), does that mean you can hear His voice?
  - ❖ What are a few examples of God speaking to your thoughts to strengthen, encourage, comfort or guide you?
  - ❖ Will a few people share the words God spoke to you (p. 21)?

Prayer:

[Put on some worship music in the background and then gather around and lay hands on and pray for those who want to receive the baptism of the Holy Spirit and receive the gift of tongues.]

As we pray, those who already have a prayer language, please pray out loud quietly in your prayer language, and those who are ready to receive can simply open your mouth and speak whatever comes out of your mouth that isn't your own language.

Since it is strange, you may want to start out by repeating sentence-by-sentence someone else's prayer language until you have confidence to believe for your own.

If you are too nervous or are experiencing doubts, as soon as you get home tonight open your mouth by faith and let the words come. You will quickly see it isn't gibberish, but is a beautiful language. Pray every chance you can in your new language—in the car, while getting ready for work, exercising or doing chores—and let God pray through you!

Practice in a Safe Place:

#1: Break up into groups of two and ask God to give you words of love for the other person in your group.

#2: Pray for any needs either of you might have.

Week 2:

We're Listening

Week 2: We're Listening
Quick Version

Prayer:

Dear Father, help me to see people through your eyes. They are often hurting, lonely, confused and harassed by the devil. Show me how to treasure those you treasure with my words, actions and facial expressions. Allow me to be a carrier of your love and kindness in every encounter with strangers, family and friends.

You Can Do It: (Don't forget to write or audio-record your encounters.)

Pray silently for everyone you pass or interact with all week.

Chit-chat with strangers to let them know they are seen and important.

Keep praying silently, but also begin to chit-chat and talk more intentionally with people wherever you go. Point out things about them that you like—something they are wearing, their hair, their smile, their friendliness or other positive personality traits you notice. You might be amazed how many people never hear words of affirmation or kindness spoken to them. Your fears will continue to dissolve as you see that people just want to be loved!

Reading:

No More No pp. 23-35 (Chapter 2—We're Listening)

Reading time: 18 minutes

Notes, comments or questions from your reading, and ideas for applying it to your life:

Week 2: We're Listening
Going Deeper

Prayer:

Dear Father, help me to see people through your eyes. They are often hurting, lonely, confused and harassed by the devil. Show me how to treasure those you treasure with my words, actions and facial expressions. Allow me to be a carrier of your love and kindness in every encounter with strangers, family and friends.

You Can Do It: (Don't forget to write or audio-record your encounters.)

Pray silently for everyone you pass or interact with all week.

Chit-chat with strangers to let them know they are seen and important.

Keep praying silently, but also begin to chit-chat and talk more intentionally with people wherever you go. Point out things about them that you like—something they are wearing, their hair, their smile, their friendliness or other positive personality traits you notice. You might be amazed how many people never hear words of affirmation or kindness spoken to them. Your fears will continue to dissolve as you see that people just want to be loved!

Section 1—You've Gotta Know This

Before going any further in this study, it is vital that you understand God's passionate love for us as people. God loves being our best Friend and being intimately involved in every area of our lives!

If you don't believe this, please don't try to express God's heart to people until you do. I recently heard a Christian say that God happily throws people into hell, and it made me weep. Yes, people will spend eternity in hell apart from God, but that isn't God's will or His choice.

Read:

No More No pp. 23-25 (Chapter 2—We're Listening)

Verse: (Pray it as you say it 5 times.)

"God is light; in Him there is no darkness at all."
1 John 1:5

1. What happens to darkness when a bright light is turned on?

2. Read 1 Timothy 6:15b-16. Why do you think God's light is unapproachable?

3. Read Psalm 5:4. Who can't dwell with sin?

   If we tried to take our unforgiven sin with us to heaven, where the fullness of God's presence dwells, we would be destroyed along with our sin. God, in His fullness, cannot dwell with sin because sin is the absence of God (the absence of light), and He can't be absent from Himself (from light). That is why Jesus became God in the flesh so that He could reach us in our sin. He came as the Light of the world!

4. I am sorry if I am being confusing, but the bottom line is that God is not happily throwing people into hell. He has no choice but to separate them from Himself, and the blessings of His presence, if they still carry their sins once they die.

Response:

In a few sentences, write how you might explain to someone why they can't take their sins to heaven and why Jesus came to take the punishment for their sins: (You will probably share this truth often when you talk with people, so keep it simple.)

Section 2—God Speaks Through Thoughts & Promptings

Read:

No More No pp. 25-29 (Chapter 2—We're Listening)

Verse: (Pray it as you say it 5 times.)

"But the Counselor, the Holy Spirit, whom the Father will send in my name, will teach you all things and will remind you of everything I have said to you."

John 14:26

1. The Holy Spirit wouldn't be able to teach, remind and lead you if He couldn't speak to your thoughts and prompt you to do things (or not do things). As I mentioned in the reading, even Jesus and the Father spoke most often through their thoughts. This is why it is crucial that you tune into what the Holy Spirit is speaking to your thoughts—for you and for others.

2. Read John 8:28 and 12:49-50. What example did Jesus set for you?

3. Aren't you glad God didn't suddenly become mute just because He wrote a bestseller? If He counts the hairs on your head, you can bet He wants to speak to you about every detail of your life. That's what a loving Father does.

   What problems or situations are you facing right now where you need God to speak to your thoughts to give you wisdom, direction, comfort or encouragement? (Write your situation and His response.)

   God didn't leave you alone with only the roadmap that He wrote for you (the Bible). He is your GPS, constantly talking to you every step of the way!

4. Listening for thoughts, promptings and urgings that God has for others is no different than listening for what God has for you. When you are in a checkout line, working out in the gym, at work or at school, and you are interacting with someone, you can ask God, "What do you have for this person? What words, wisdom, insights or healing do you want to give them?"

5. The devil will tell you that you can't hear God's voice because if he can silence God's voice in your life, he can seriously hinder you and make you of little impact on the earth.

   Let's look at the truths from God's Word to overcome the devil's lies. What does each of these incredible verses say?

   1 Corinthians 2:16

   John 8:47

   Jeremiah 33:3

   John 10:27

   Mark 13:11

   You can hear the Father's voice speaking to your thoughts because you are His beloved child!

   Remember that the words He speaks to you will never contradict the Bible (that's how cults get started). They will be specific words to strengthen, encourage and comfort you or others.

Section 3—God Speaks Through Peace or Uneasiness

Read:

No More No pp. 29-33 [top line on p. 33] (Chapter 2—We're Listening)

Verse: (Pray it as you say it 5 times.)

"And the peace of God, which transcends all understanding, will guard your hearts and your minds in Christ Jesus."

Philippians 4:7

1. The angels weren't kidding when they declared at Jesus' birth *"Glory to God in the highest, and on earth peace, goodwill toward men"* (Luke 2:14 KJV). Jesus' coming to earth made it possible for us to have peace—peace *with* God and peace *in* God.

   Once you are in God's peace as a born-again Christian, it's important to stay in that peace by fixing your eyes on Jesus and following His leading every step of the way. When you do, God can guard your heart and your mind, and He can protect you.

   Read Romans 8:5-6. What are the results of setting your mind on what the Spirit desires for you?

2. A sense of peace or a sense of uneasiness are two ways the Holy Spirit communicates to give you a *yes* or a *no* in everything you do. Can you think of an example when God gave you a sense of uneasiness about something, and later you saw why He was stopping you?

   (I ignored the Holy Spirit's uneasiness before I headed to meet some very special people one day, and when I was 1½ hours from home, my transmission went out in my van. I should have listened to that "check" or lack of peace. God knew my transmission was failing!)

3. Can you think of an example when you had a peace about doing something that didn't make sense in the natural?

What happened?

4. Peace or uneasiness are also fantastic tools the Holy Spirit has provided to guide you as you begin listening for God's voice for others.

   Read Acts 16:6-7. These may have been examples of lack of peace in their spirits to guide them. What happened in each instance?

   Side note: Notice that God's Spirit is referred to as the Holy Spirit in the first verse and the Spirit of Jesus in the second verse. This is further proof that Jesus is God. They are one and the same!

5. It is vital to understand the difference between feeling uneasiness coming from the Holy Spirit and feeling fear coming from you or the devil. As you begin saying *yes* to God's promptings, you will probably feel fearful until you see that you can trust God and relax. Fear is different from lack of peace. You may feel fear about the consequences, but still have a sense of peace that you are doing the right thing no matter the cost.

Response:

As you are pushing yourself to speak with strangers this week—affirming them and chatting about various topics—pay attention to the difference between fear and a lack of peace. Force yourself to begin speaking even when you feel fearful, and then pay attention to what that fear feels like.

If God gives you a negative, yucky feeling about some decision or action this week, pay attention to what that feels like also.

Once you recognize the difference, you can silence the devil's lies when you feel fear and tune into God's voice when you feel a lack of peace. God uses this method of communicating in every area of your life, so ask Him to make the difference clear to you.

Section 4—God Speaks Through Pictures and Pain

Read:

No More No pp. 33-35 (Chapter 2—We're Listening)

Verse:

"During the night Paul had a vision of a man of Macedonia standing and begging him, "Come over to Macedonia and help us."

Acts 16:9

1. God has always spoken through visions or pictures to one degree or another because it's a great way to get someone's attention and easy for the human mind to remember. God used a vision of a man of Macedonia to make Paul aware of the need there, and He wants to show us pictures and visions in order to make us aware of needs or things He is doing in someone's life.

   Can you think of a dream or picture God gave you that stuck in your memory?

2. Since we aren't face to face with God, we still benefit from visions, pictures and dreams when God wants to tell us something. He knows a picture is worth a thousand words.

   Read Joel 2:28 and Acts 2:16-20. What does it say?

   Note: It is important to realize that Joel wasn't being literal in the sense that only young men can see visions and only old men can dream dreams. Paul wasn't an especially young man when he became a believer, yet he saw visions *and* dreamed dreams until he died as an older man. Joel's point was that no one was excluded because God would pour out His Spirit on everyone no matter their age or gender.

3. There are different types of visions. The types of visions I see are faint pictures in my mind's eye—almost like sketches. Sometimes they just pop into my head, but most of the time I have to ask for and expect them before I see them.

Expectation is the key in every area of our walk of faith. If you believe God *wants* to give you pictures—and that God *can* give you pictures—then your faith will open the door for Him to give you pictures. Unfortunately, your unbelief and doubt will shut the door because Jesus said, *"According to your faith be it done to you" (Matthew 9:29).*

Do you struggle with believing your loving Father wants to show you pictures to bless you and others? How can you overcome that lie?

4. Feeling pain temporarily in your body is another way God may let you know that someone around you needs prayer for that particular issue, so pay attention to your body and ask those around you if they need healing when you feel body parts start to ache randomly. Has this ever happened to you? Did you pray for someone?

The Bible doesn't specifically mention this type of communication, but it doesn't conflict with how God works or the rest of Scripture. God had the Old Testament prophets often do a lot of weird things to get the people's attention, so giving you pain in your shoulder, hand or ankle for a few minutes makes perfect sense.

Remember, too, that most of the things Jesus did while on the earth were not written down. There is so much we don't know about His time on the earth. He or the disciples may have felt pain when someone needed healed. Read John 21:25. What does it say?

Response:

I would encourage you to take God out of the box that we often put Him in and let Him be BIG in you and through you. Tune into the subtle ways He is communicating through thoughts, promptings, peace, uneasiness, pictures or pain. You may be amazed at how much He wants to say!

Chapter Highlights: (*No More No* p. 35)

Read the Chapter Highlights and Application for review and inspiration.

Week 2: Group Wrap-Up

Group Session #3

- Let's pray.

- **Group Outreaches:** Let's plan a time for our group to go out together. We will break up into groups of two and ask God to highlight people with His love, then express that love and ask if they have any prayer needs (and pray right then if they don't mind.)

- Last week's "You Can Do It":
  - ❖ How did it go praying silently for people and being intentional about speaking with people, making them feel special and important?
  - ❖ Did it change anything in you? Did any fears diminish?

- Next week's "You Can Do It":
  - ❖ Continue to pray silently for people you pass and interact with, and continue to be intentional to talk with strangers, making them feel important and affirming them whenever possible.
  - ❖ This week also ask God to highlight at least one stranger with His love and tell them something like:
    - ▪ "God just highlighted you to me because He wants you to know how special you are to Him."
    - ▪ "I was praying God would bless you as I passed you, and He impressed on me how much He loves you."

    Then open your mouth and trust God to give you more words of love and affirmation, perhaps telling them how God views them and the good things He has in store. (Remember to write your encounters in the back of this study guide or in your journal, or to audio or video record them.)

- Section 1 Discussion: You've Gotta Know This
  - ❖ Read 1 John 1:5.
  - ❖ What does this verse mean in relation to sin and darkness?
  - ❖ Two or three people share what you wrote in the response on p. 29 where you explained why we can't take our sins with us to heaven.

36

- Section 2 Discussion: God Speaks Through Thoughts & Promptings
  - ❖ Read John 14:26.
  - ❖ Could a God who is silent do what this verse says?
  - ❖ Why do you think the devil is trying so hard to convince the church that God is now mute and unable to speak with His children?
  - ❖ Five different people read these verses out loud and briefly share insights as a group:
    - ▪ 1 Corinthians 2:16
    - ▪ John 8:47
    - ▪ Jeremiah 33:3
    - ▪ John 10:27
    - ▪ Mark 13:11
  - ❖ Let's have a few people share a story of how God spoke to your thoughts or prompted you to say or do something.

- Section 3 Discussion: God Speaks Through Peace or Uneasiness
  - ❖ Read Philippians 4:7.
  - ❖ God protects and guides us with His peace or a lack of peace. Will several people please share stories of being guided by peace or a lack of peace?
  - ❖ When you were being bold in talking with people this week, what were the differences you discovered between fear and a lack of peace?
  - ❖ Read Romans 8:5-6.
  - ❖ Why is it vital to fix our eyes on Jesus and walk in the leading of the Spirit?

- Section 4 Discussion: God Speaks Through Pictures and Pain
  - ❖ Read Acts 16:9 and 2:16-20 and discuss.
  - ❖ Since we are in the last days, we are still hearing from God through dreams and visions. Let's have several people briefly share visions in your mind's eye that God gave you for yourself or for others and how it helped.
  - ❖ Has anyone felt pain in your body as a prompting to pray for someone in pain? If so, what happened?

[Important note to read to the group before you start the practice]: These group exercises are a way to push yourself out of your comfort zone and learn how to love people more than you love your reputation. Philippians 2:7 says that Jesus made himself of no reputation, and you and I have the incredible privilege of following Jesus' example and laying down our desire to protect our reputation.

Every time you need to step out by faith, do three things:

1. **Silence the devil's lies** telling you that you can't hear God's voice or be used by God.

2. **Speak God's truth.** I have the mind of Christ. The Father's sheep hear His voice and I am His sheep. I have the same power that raised Christ from the dead dwelling in me. Jesus said I would do greater things than He did....

3. **Expect God to be BIG through you.** I am simply a water hose for God to flow His gifts and power through! According to my faith be it unto me!

If it appears someone misses a word or impression, give them a high-five and celebrate with them because they were willing to risk being wrong in order to learn how to be right.

If someone gives you a word that you aren't sure about, set it on a "shelf" and ask God to confirm it in other ways if it is Him talking.

1 Thessalonians 5:19-21 says, *"Do not put out the Spirit's fire; do not treat prophecies with contempt. Test everything. Hold on to the good."*

Most of all, simply relax and have fun!

Let's pray before we start.

Practice in a Safe Place:

#1: As a group, we will take turns having someone be "it," and have three or four people speak words of love from the Father's heart for them as they feel prompted. Ask God for pictures in your mind's eye, along with the meaning of the pictures. Take risks. It is ok to be wrong! Once the person has received three or four words, pick someone else.

#2: Break up into groups of two or three and share words of love from the Father for each other, and then pray for any specific needs you may have.

Week 3:

Yes, Lord!

Week 3: Yes, Lord!
Quick Version

Prayer:

Dear Father, help me to trust you with my "Yes!"

You Can Do It: (Don't forget to write or audio-record your encounters.)

Pray silently for everyone you pass or interact with all week.

Chit-chat with strangers to let them know they are seen and important.

Tell one stranger that God highlighted them with His love.

You might say:

- "God just highlighted you because He wants you to know how special you are to Him."
- "I was praying that God would bless you, and He impressed on me how much He loves you."

Then open your mouth and trust God to give you words of love and affirmation, perhaps telling them how God views them and the good things He has in store for them.

Reading:

No More No pp. 37-53 (Chapter 3—Yes, Lord!)

No More No pp. 107-113 (First half of Chapter 7—March Boldly)

Reading time for both sections: 21 minutes and 8½ minutes

Notes, comments or questions from your reading, and ideas for applying it to your life:

Week 3: Yes, Lord!
Going Deeper

Prayer:

Dear Father, help me to trust you with my "Yes!"

You Can Do It: (Don't forget to write or audio-record your encounters.)

Pray silently for everyone you pass or interact with all week.

Chit-chat with strangers to let them know they are seen and important.

Tell one stranger that God highlighted them with His love.

You might say:

- "God just highlighted you because He wants you to know how special you are to Him."
- "I was praying that God would bless you, and He impressed on me how much He loves you."

Then open your mouth and trust God to give you words of love and affirmation, perhaps telling them how God views them and the good things He has in store for them.

Section 1—Trusting God with Your "Yes!"

Read:

No More No pp. 37-43 (Chapter 3—Yes, Lord!)

Verse: (Pray it as you say it 5 times.)

"Trust in the Lord with all your heart, and lean not on your own understanding; in all your ways acknowledge Him, and He shall direct your paths."

Proverbs 3:5-6 (NKJV)

1. Write down what God shows you about these verses in relation to saying *yes* to God's promptings:

2. Do you ever feel like a two year old telling God *no*? In what ways?

3. The bottom line of all our issues in life—whether depression, anger or disobedience to God's voice—is that we simply don't trust God.

On page 42 of *No More No*, I mention that even though God is perfect in love and wisdom, we are often afraid to share God's words and obey His promptings because "we don't fully trust our Father. Satan tells us we'll look stupid, say the wrong thing or ruin our reputation, so we trust his lies rather than the Father's love—and we remain silent."

What lies of Satan are you trusting when you allow fear to stop you from obeying God's promptings?

What truths about God's love and character counter those lies?

4. Hebrews 5:8 (NLT) says that *"Even though Jesus was God's Son, he learned obedience from the things he suffered."* The only way to learn obedience is to obey—being willing to suffer for the one you obey. Just as a two year old learns obedience by obeying, you will learn obedience by obeying and allowing God to prove Himself to you.

Most of the time you will find that obedience to God's will doesn't cause much suffering, but even if it does, especially as things get worse on the earth, you can entrust yourself to the God who loves you passionately. He will love you, surround you and fill you with inexpressible joy as you do His will on the earth!

Response:

"When they hurled their insults at him [Jesus], he did not retaliate; when he suffered, he made no threats. Instead, he entrusted himself to him who judges justly" (1 Peter 2:23). Ask God to help you entrust yourself to Him as you take up your cross and obey Him no matter the cost.

Section 2—Your "Yes, Lord" Declaration

Spend time in prayer, thinking about the things that keep you from saying *yes* to the King of Kings and Lord of Lords who loves you perfectly. (Read again pp. 42-43 of *No More No.*) Then write your own "Yes, Lord!" Declaration.

(You may want to photocopy this page, or type up a separate page, and hang your declaration on your fridge, mirror or somewhere at work or school to remind you.)

Notes, thoughts or prayers:

Section 3—God's Parcel Service (GPS)

Read:

No More No pp. 43-52 (Chapter 3—Yes, Lord!)

Verse: (Pray it as you say it 6 times—change it up a bit.)

"For we are God's handiwork, created in Christ Jesus to do good works, which God prepared in advance for us to do."

Ephesians 2:10

1. Good news! You don't have to prepare your own good works. You get to leave manufacturing, jump in your delivery truck and deliver the gifts God has prepared in advance for you to do. You can forget formulas, methods and striving to figure out what to say. Instead, as an employee of God's Parcel Service (GPS), you get to tune into God's voice and find out what He wants to say and do.

   What are some formulas or methods you have tried in the past to share the Good News with people, and why were they hard to use?

2. Joining God's Parcel Service takes all the stress and pressure off of you. Psalm 81:10 says, *"Open wide your mouth and I will fill it."* What does that mean?

   There are many times when God makes someone stand out to me and I know He has something for them, but I don't have a clue what He wants to say. I have to choose to open my mouth and begin speaking, trusting that God wants to fill my mouth even more than I want Him to fill it. In the natural, it almost feels like I am making it up, but it is amazing that when your faith is in God and not in yourself, He is free to show up and show off.

3. Jesus worked for God's Parcel Service to show us that we are called and equipped for that same job. He said in John 14:12: *"Very truly I tell you, whoever believes in me will do the works I have been doing, and they will do even greater things than these, because I am going to the Father."*

What were the works Jesus did?

According to this verse, what is the only requirement you have in order to do those same works and greater works?

God Encounters:

As you read my stories, write down what works God prepared and gave through me. (And make notes of tips on delivering gifts in love.)

"Forgotten Items" (pp. 45-46)

"Sleeping on the Job" (pp. 46-48)

"Sopping with Sweat" (pp. 48-49)

"Wisdom Teeth and Heavenly Wisdom" (pp. 49-51)

"My Big Book" (pp. 51-52)

Section 4—Stepping Out on the Water

Read:

No More No pp. 107-113 (First half of Chapter 7—March Boldly)

Verse: (Pray it as you say it 6 times.)

"'Lord, if it's you,' Peter replied, 'tell me to come to you on the water.'
'Come,' he said."

Matthew 14:28-29

1. In what ways is God asking you to get out of your safe "boat" and step out on the water?

2. When the Holy Spirit asked me to stand up in the theatre that first time, I was literally shaking. But every time you step out into new levels of obedience, fear diminishes and your trust in God grows.

   Two years after this theatre story, the Holy Spirit asked me to stand up again in the theatre and offer to pray for people after watching "The Case for Christ." That time I only felt fearful for a few seconds and then I was fine because I knew God would take care of me and bless people in the process. (No one got saved, but a young Christian couple came and stood with me and asked me to help them become more bold for Jesus.)

   Can you think of examples where you have seen your fears diminishing and your trust growing as you began stepping out on the water?

3. Ron's concern for the loud and somewhat chaotic situation in which I shared Jesus that first time in the theatre was an issue to pray about, but it is important to realize that when God asks you to do something, it may not always be under ideal circumstances. You will have to be willing to say *yes* and trust God with the outcome.

   Can you think of some examples in the Bible where things were chaotic for Jesus or the disciples yet they still chose to obey God?

4. Learning how to honor your spouse as you work for GPS is another important factor this story addresses. Although Ron is good at hearing God's voice, when I first began this lifestyle he wasn't very comfortable, so I was more careful to keep interactions with people to a minimum when we were together. But as Ron watched my interactions and heard my stories, his heart softened to the concept and he began to join in at times.

   Do you have a spouse who might struggle, or is struggling, with your desire to express God's words, love and truth wherever you go?

   What do you feel the Holy Spirit is telling you to do about it?

   God will give you creative ideas and orchestrate situations so that you can be His hands, voice and feet, and still love and honor your spouse. (Just don't use your spouse as an excuse to say *no* to God's promptings. If God prompts you to speak, He will work things out with your spouse.)

Chapter Highlights: (*No More No* pp. 52-53)

Read the Chapter Highlights and Application for review and inspiration.

Week 3: Group Wrap-Up

Group Session #4

- Let's pray.

- [Discuss past or upcoming outreaches as a group.]

- Last week's "You Can Do It":
  - ❖ Last week we continued to pray silently for people and to be more intentional with starting conversations to make people feel loved. How is that going?
  - ❖ We added in the goal of asking God to highlight at least one stranger with His love, and then we were to express those words of love. What obstacles did you face and how did you overcome the devil's lies, doubts and fears?
  - ❖ What were your encounters?

- Next week's "You Can Do It":
  - ❖ Continue to pray silently for people you pass and interact with, and be intentional to talk with strangers, making them feel important and loved.
  - ❖ This week again ask God to highlight at least one stranger with His love and tell them something like:
    - ▪ "God just highlighted you to me with His love. You are incredibly special to Him."
    - ▪ "I believe God speaks, and He just told me how much He loves you."

    Then open your mouth and trust God to give you more words of love and affirmation.
  - ❖ A second encounter for this week is to ask at least one person if they have any prayer needs, and then pray right then. This can be a salesman at the door, a cashier in line, a co-worker or classmate, etc. You might say:
    - ▪ "I am learning how to pray for people I interact with. Do you have any prayer needs?"
    - ▪ "I love Jesus and I love people. Are there any challenges in your life that I can pray about with you?"

    If they can't think of anything, suggest a few areas where they might be struggling such as work, family, etc.

- Section 1 Discussion: Trusting God with Your "Yes!"
  - ❖ Read Proverbs 3:5-6.
  - ❖ What do these verses teach us when it comes to saying *yes* to God's promptings?
  - ❖ What are your thoughts in regard to Julie's statement at the top of p. 43 in this study guide where she says, "The bottom line of all our issues in life—whether depression, anger or disobedience to God's voice—is that we simply don't trust God"?
  - ❖ What lies of Satan are you trusting when you say *no* to God's promptings?
  - ❖ Read Hebrews 5:8.
  - ❖ What does this verse mean?
  - ❖ If Jesus learned obedience by obeying the Father's voice no matter the suffering involved, can you trust the Father to care for and love you no matter what suffering your obedience might cause? Can you trust His love?

- Section 2 Discussion: Your "Yes, Lord!" Declaration
  - ❖ Would several people like to read your "Yes, Lord!" Declarations you wrote on p. 44 of this study guide?
  - ❖ Where did you post your Declarations as a reminder? (Your fridge? Mirror? Office? Other?)

- Section 3 Discussion: God's Parcel Service (GPS)
  - ❖ Read Ephesians 2:10 and Psalm 81:10.
  - ❖ In light of these two verses, why do we get to leave manufacturing (and following formulas) and simply deliver God's gifts?
  - ❖ Can you think of a few other ways that a UPS delivery person compares with a GPS delivery person?
  - ❖ Read John 14:12.
  - ❖ Who was the first GPS employee and what gifts did He deliver?
  - ❖ What is the one requirement for you to deliver those same gifts and greater gifts?
  - ❖ Do you have a favorite story from your notes on p. 47?

- Section 4 Discussion: Stepping Out on the Water
  - ❖ Read Matthew 14:28-29.
  - ❖ What things in your safe "boat" do you struggle to give up when Jesus says, "It is me. Come"?

❖ Do you believe your fears will keep diminishing every time Jesus keeps you from drowning? Are you willing to find out?

❖ Julie mentioned when the Holy Spirit first asked her to stand up and share Jesus in the theatre that the music during the credits was loud, making it hard for people to hear in the back. It created a slightly chaotic experience. What are a couple of examples where things were chaotic for Jesus and the disciples? Did they still obey the Father's promptings?

❖ The theatre story also brings up the importance of learning how to honor your spouse and the Holy Spirit. If you have a spouse who may not agree with your desire to step out on the water and deliver God's words, gifts, healing and love, what tips did the Lord give you to help until your spouse gets more comfortable?

❖ The biggest key is to trust that God will work things out as you sensitively follow His leading and don't shrink back.

• Let's pray before we practice, and remember to silence the devil's lies, speak the truth and expect God to be BIG in us!

Practice in a Safe Place:

Important Note: You may want to turn on your voice recorder on your phone before you receive a word so that you will have the words to go back and listen to. They can be a great encouragement!

#1: Form two circles, an inner and outer circle, with the inner circle facing the outer circle. Have the same number of people in each circle if possible. Someone will set a timer for 2 minutes and say, "Go." Then the person in the outer circle will open their mouth and ask God to fill it, giving words from the Father to strengthen, encourage or comfort the other person. Also ask for a picture and a meaning for that person. When the timer goes off, the person in the inner circle will now do the same for the person in the outer circle. When the timer goes off again, the outer circle moves one place to the right so that you are facing someone new. Repeat this until everyone in the inner circle has interacted with everyone in the outer circle.

If you still have time, team up with people from your own circle, and keep going until you have interacted with everyone in the meeting. Then discuss as a group any encouraging words and how it went.

#2: Break up into groups of two or three and pray for any prayer needs you may have.

Week 4:

What God Wants to Say & Do

Week 4: What God Wants to Say & Do
Quick Version

Prayer:

Thank you for your lavish love gifts, Holy Spirit!

You Can Do It: (Don't forget to write or audio-record your encounters.)

Pray silently for everyone you pass or interact with all week.

Chit-chat with strangers to let them know they are seen and important.

Tell one stranger that God highlighted them with His love, and then express words from God's heart.

Offer to pray for at least one stranger, and pray right then.

This can be a salesman at the door, a cashier in line, a co-worker or classmate, etc. You might say:

- "I am learning how to pray for people I interact with. Do you have any prayer needs?"
- "I love Jesus and I love people. Are there any challenges in your life that I can pray about with you?"

If they can't think of anything, suggest a few areas where they might be struggling such as work, school or family.

Reading:

No More No pp. 57-74 (Chapter 4—What God Wants to Say & Do)

No More No pp. 113-127 (Second half of Chapter 7—March Boldly)

Reading time for both sections: 23 minutes and 15 minutes

Notes, comments or questions from your reading, and ideas for applying it to your life:

Week 4: What God Wants to Say & Do
Going Deeper

Prayer:

Thank you for your lavish love gifts, Holy Spirit!

You Can Do It: (Don't forget to write or audio-record your encounters.)

Pray silently for everyone you pass or interact with all week.

Chit-chat with strangers to let them know they are seen and important.

Tell one stranger that God highlighted them with His love, and then express words from God's heart.

Offer to pray for at least one stranger, and pray right then.

This can be a salesman at the door, a cashier in line, a co-worker or classmate, etc. You might say:

- "I am learning how to pray for people I interact with. Do you have any prayer needs?"
- "I love Jesus and I love people. Are there any challenges in your life that I can pray about with you?"

If they can't think of anything, suggest a few areas where they might be struggling such as work, school or family.

Section 1—God's Lavish Love Gifts

Read:

No More No pp. 57-61 (Chapter 4—What God Wants to Say & Do)

Verse: (Pray it as you say it 5 times.)

"How great is the love the Father has lavished on us, that we should be called children of God!"

1 John 3:1

1. One of the amazing wonders of being a child of God and having His Spirit living *in* you is that God gets to lavish His love *on* you! List several ways that the Father lavishes His love on you.

2. Read 1 Corinthians 12:4-11 and list the nine love gifts God wants to lavish on you to bless you and others.

3. Verse 6 says that God *"works all things in all persons,"* and verse 7 says, "To each one is given the manifestation of the Spirit." What does this mean? (Look up the word "manifestation.")

The gifts of the Spirit are for everyone who receives them by faith. God is no respecter of persons. His Spirit is available for all of us!

4. What does 1 Thessalonians 5:19 say we are not to do, and in what ways have you possibly done that?

Response:

If you have grieved, quenched or forbidden the Holy Spirit from flowing His lavish love gifts to you and through you, pour out your heart to Him right now, asking Him to wash away the lies, doubts and unbelief that are hindering you from receiving the gifts God has for you. Write down your prayer of choosing to trust His gift-giving wisdom and love:

Section 2—Communication Gifts

Read:

No More No pp. 61-63, 68-73 (Chapter 4—What God Wants to Say & Do)

Verse: (Pray it as you say it 5 times.)

"We speak of God's secret wisdom…"

1 Corinthians 2:7

1. **Words of Wisdom**

   God uses us to impart not only the secret wisdom of salvation, but every aspect of God's wisdom to our world. Many people read 1 Corinthians 2:9, which is a quote from the Old Testament, but they forget to keep reading verse 10, which is our New Testament promise. Read these verses and explain what they mean:

   God's Spirit is constantly revealing His thoughts and wisdom to you because you have the mind of Christ. He wants you to reach into your GPS truck daily and share God's thoughts and wisdom with your world.

2. **Words of Knowledge**

   A word of knowledge is information the Holy Spirit gives you about someone else to prove that He is real and loves them passionately. Two days ago I was walking into the grocery store and God highlighted a young man. I had a faint picture of him in a race car on a race track, so I opened my mouth, trusting God would explain the meaning as I spoke. What popped into my head was that he felt like he was going in circles and struggling for direction. Then I shared that I saw Jesus getting in the car with Him to lead and guide him. He was amazed and flabbergasted because this word of knowledge and a few other words I shared were apparently very accurate. Not only were these words of knowledge exactly what He needed to hear, but he had been praying a few days earlier for a sign from God!

Can you think of a word of knowledge that someone gave to you or that you gave to someone else that had a big impact?

3. **Words of Prophecy** (Skip over and read pp. 68-73 in *No More No.*)
1 Corinthians 14:1 gives you two vital instructions for life: *"Follow the way of love and eagerly desire spiritual gifts, especially the gift of prophecy."*

Everything you do must be bathed in love, and if you truly love people you have to step out of your comfort zone and give people the gifts God has made available for them—especially prophecy. True love won't leave gifts from God rotting and useless in your GPS truck.

Prophecy encompasses words of wisdom and knowledge, but it also includes things coming up in the future or a victory the Lord has declared for someone. Read again 1 Corinthians 14:3-4. What is the goal of prophecy?

Read 1 Corinthians 14:31-33. Will God force words out of your mouth that you can't control?

Verse 32 says, *"The spirits of prophets are subject to the control of prophets."* This means that not only are you responsible to keep things orderly, but that you have the ability to stop or release the flow of God. Every time He asks you to speak, you can say *yes* or *no*.

Response:

As in everything in life, you have free will. God will let you obey His voice or ignore it. He'll let you deliver His gifts or leave people giftless.

Since words of wisdom, knowledge and prophecy are all love gifts for you and for others, begin today to expect God to speak through you—and then open your mouth and let Him fill it. In this world that is spinning out of control, people desperately need to hear from God!

Section 3—Physical Manifestation & Discerning Gifts

Read:

No More No pp. 63-68 (Chapter 4—What God Wants to Say & Do)

Verse: (Pray it as you say it 5 times.)

The disciples couldn't cast the demon out of a boy, so Jesus had to rebuke the demon. They asked Jesus, *"'Why couldn't we drive it out?' He replied, 'Because you have so little faith. I tell you the truth, if you have faith as small as a mustard seed, you can say to this mountain, 'Move from here to there' and it will move. Nothing will be impossible for you.'"*

Matthew 17:19-21

1. **Faith, Healing and Miracles**
   It is heartbreaking to me how Satan has convinced most Christians that God wants them sick. If this were the case, God would have given us at least one example in the Bible of Jesus refusing to heal someone because He wanted them to grow through their suffering rather than be healed from their suffering. We don't have even one example of this. On the contrary, what does the Bible say?

   Matthew 8:16

   Acts 10:38

   Not only did Jesus heal all who came to Him with faith for healing, but He operated out of the power of the same Holy Spirit who lives in you and me. Jesus didn't come to just *wow* us with miracles and then leave us helpless. What does Ephesians 1:18-20 tell us we have?

   If you and I aren't operating in the same power Jesus did, does that mean Jesus lied or does that mean we need to figure out how to grow our faith and silence the lies and doubts of the devil?

   What does Mark 11:23-24 say?

Most Christians hate to quote Jesus when it comes to faith for healing and miracles because Satan falsely attaches guilt to Jesus' words. But once you understand that you simply need the filter of your mind cleaned out from the lies of the enemy, you won't feel condemnation, but tremendous hope. Jesus already did His part and paid for our healing on the cross, and the rest is up to us—to believe and receive!

On September 11, 2016 I was determined to take back what the enemy had stolen from me and to quit relying on doctors, medicine and supplements. I spent hours a day renewing my mind by reading the gospels and soaking teachings and healing testimonies by Andrew Wommack and others until I finally understood deep in my heart that healing was already mine. And then—praise God—the healings and miracles began. My thyroid, head injury, back issues, hormones, digestive problems—and more—were healed! God's will had not changed—He always wanted me well—but my faith had changed!

If I had believed that my faith couldn't grow and that I didn't have authority over sickness, I would still be sick and in pain. (You can see my healing stories on our website videos at CrazyAboutYou.org.)

The books and free video teachings by Andrew Wommack entitled *God Wants You Well, The Believer's Authority* and *You've Already Got It* were key to my breakthrough (and explain issues like Paul's thorn in the flesh). There are still a few mountains I am speaking to, but I am well on my way to understanding that Jesus truly gave us authority over every mountain, sickness and disease the devil throws our way!

2. **Distinguishing of Spirits, Tongues, Interpretation of Tongues**
   Read Ephesians 6:12. Why is it crucial that we discern (or distinguish) when God is speaking to us and when the devil or our flesh are speaking to us?

The demonic realm is constantly lying, but we have authority to silence those lies and speak the truth instead.

I am out of space, but feel free to read my earlier comments in week 1 about the amazing gift of speaking in tongues, and then silence the lies of the devil that try to keep you from using this life-changing gift!

Section 4—March Boldly

Read:

No More No pp. 113-127 (Second half of Chapter 7—March Boldly)

Verse: (Pray it as you say it 5 times.)

"I long to see you so that I may impart to you some spiritual gift to make you strong—"

Romans 1:11

For each of the stories, write down the spiritual gifts that were imparted, how those gifts may have strengthened the receiver and any helpful tips you discovered to aid you in delivering your own gifts.

"Email Plunge" (pp. 114-117)

"Costco Encounters" (pp. 117-119)

"Chasing the Cane" (pp. 119-120)

"Working Prayers" (pp. 120-121)

"A Miss and Ice" (pp. 121-123)

"Working with the Comforter" (pp. 124-125)

"Joseph and an Egg Encounter" (pp. 125-127)

"Prayers for Grace (p. 127)

Chapter Highlights: (*No More No* p. 74)

Read the Chapter Highlights and Application for review and inspiration.

Week 4: Group Wrap-Up

Group Session #5

- Let's pray.

- [Discuss past or upcoming outreaches as a group.]

- Last week's "You Can Do It":
  - ❖ Are you noticing your heart change as you continue to pray silently for people, and as you are more intentional about talking with people to make them feel special?
  - ❖ What are your stories of expressing God's love and offering to pray for people?

- Next week's "You Can Do It":
  - ❖ Continue to pray silently for people you pass and interact with, and be intentional to talk with strangers, making them feel important and loved.
  - ❖ This week ask God to highlight at least two strangers with His love. Express God's heart and then pray for them.
  - ❖ If you are feeling brave and ready to trust God to fill your mouth, ask God for a picture, a word of knowledge or something coming up in their future.

- Section 1 Discussion: God's Lavish Love Gifts
  - ❖ Read 1 John 3:1 and 1 Corinthians 12:4-11.
  - ❖ What are the nine gifts God has lavished on us by the Spirit?
  - ❖ In light of these two passages, what are your thoughts in regard to Julie's statement at the bottom of p. 59 of *No More No*: "God's lavish love poured in us transforms our lives. God's lavish love poured through us transforms our world."
  - ❖ Read 1 Thessalonians 5:19.
  - ❖ Are there ways you have quenched or stifled the Holy Spirit, and if so, what can you do to stop hindering what He wants to do through you?

- Section 2 Discussion: Communication Gifts
  - ❖ What are the three communication gifts from 1 Corinthians 12:8-10?
  - ❖ 1 Corinthians 2:7a says, *"We speak of God's secret wisdom."* Salvation is the most important wisdom we need to impart, but

what other "secret wisdom" does God want us to impart wherever we go? (Hint: See previous question.)

❖ Read 1 Corinthians 2:9-10.

❖ What does this passage mean?

❖ A word of knowledge is information that the Holy Spirit gives you about someone else to prove that He is real and that He loves them passionately.

❖ Can you think of a word of knowledge someone gave you, or that you gave to someone else, that had a big impact?

❖ Read 1 Corinthians 14:1-4.

❖ Why should we eagerly desire to prophesy?

❖ Read 1 Corinthians 14:32. Does God force you to speak?

- Section 3 Discussion: Physical Manifestation and Discerning Gifts

    ❖ What are the three physical manifestation gifts from 1 Corinthians 12:8-10?

    ❖ Read Matthew 17:14-20.

    ❖ How does this passage prove that just because someone is sick, it isn't God's will for them to stay sick?

    ❖ Read Matthew 6:9-10.

    ❖ Jesus told us to pray for God's will to be done on earth because, due to our free will, God's will is often not done. Jesus makes it clear that His will is being done in heaven, so we can look to heaven to see what His will is for the earth. Is there sickness in heaven?

    ❖ Read Matthew 8:16.

    ❖ How many of the sick and demon possessed did Jesus heal?

    ❖ If God's will was to keep some people sick, then Jesus was not walking in God's will because He healed everyone who had faith to be healed.

    ❖ Read Mark 11:23-24.

    ❖ If your mountain of sickness or disease hasn't moved yet, you shouldn't feel condemned, but rather excited that as you renew your mind and silence the lies and doubts of the enemy, you will see those mountains move. Jesus is not a liar!

    ❖ Has anyone experienced healing breakthrough as you have renewed your mind?

    ❖ What are the final three gifts listed in point #2 on p. 61 of this study?

    ❖ Do you have any comments or questions about them?

- Section 4 Discussion: March Boldly
  - ❖ Read Romans 1:11.
  - ❖ Why is it vital that we impart and deliver spiritual gifts?
  - ❖ Did you pick up helpful tips in Julie's stories from the 2nd half of Chapter 7—March Boldly? (See pp. 62-63 in this guide.)
- Let's pray.

Before you step out by faith:

1. **Silence the devil's lies** telling you that you can't hear God's voice or be used by God.

2. **Speak God's truth.** I have the mind of Christ. The Father's sheep hear His voice and I am His sheep. I have the same power that raised Christ from the dead dwelling in me. Jesus said I would do greater things than He did....

3. **Expect God to be BIG through you.** I am simply a water hose for God to flow His gifts and power through! According to my faith be it unto me!

Practice in a Safe Place:

#1: Half of the group needs to stand in a line, side by side so that you can't see behind you. (You may want to close your eyes at first.) Then everyone else come and stand behind someone, but don't say anything so they don't know who you are. Take turns one at a time (and out loud so that everyone can hear) giving a word to the person standing behind you. Remember, it isn't about confidence in you, but confidence in your big God! God wants to strengthen, encourage and comfort others through you, so take risks and try to hear specific details. When everyone is done, turn around and discuss with the person what the word meant to you. Share with the whole group if you would like.

Then the group who was behind will now stand in a row in front, repeating the whole process.

This is a safe place to take risks, so don't let it stop you if you mess up. Keep silencing the demonic lies that say you can't hear God's voice, and ask God to help you believe that you can! *"According to your faith be it done to you" (Matthew 9:29).*

#2: Break up into groups of two or three to pray for one another. Practice hearing God's voice as you minister to one another.

Week 5:

Step Out in Confidence

Week 5: Step Out in Confidence
Quick Version

Prayer:

Thank you, Holy Spirit, that my confidence is not in me, but in You!

You Can Do It: (Don't forget to write or audio-record your encounters.)

Pray silently for everyone you pass or interact with all week.

Chit-chat with strangers to let them know they are seen and important.

Tell at least two strangers that God highlighted them with His love, and then express words from God's heart.

Try taking a risk and asking God for a picture, a word of knowledge or something coming up in their future. Then offer to pray, and pray right then.

Reading:

No More No pp. 75-89 (Chapter 5—Step Out in Confidence)

No More No pp. 129-137 (First half of Chapter 8—Still Marching)

Reading time for both sections: 21 minutes and 12 minutes

Notes, comments or questions from your reading, and ideas for applying it to your life:

Week 5: Step Out in Confidence
Going Deeper

Prayer:

Thank you, Holy Spirit, that my confidence is not in me, but in You!

You Can Do It: (Don't forget to write or audio-record your encounters.)

Pray silently for everyone you pass or interact with all week.

Chit-chat with strangers to let them know they are seen and important.

Tell at least two strangers that God highlighted them with His love, and then express words from God's heart.

Try taking a risk and asking God for a picture, a word of knowledge or something coming up in their future. Then offer to pray, and pray right then.

Section 1—You Can Hear God

Read:

No More No pp. 75-77 (Chapter 5—Step Out in Confidence)

Verse: (Pray it as you say it 10 times or more to memorize it.)

"He who belongs to God hears what God says."
John 8:47

1. According to John 8:47 who can hear what God says?

   Do you belong to God?

   So can you hear what God says?

2. The tendency is to look for some special key in *No More No* or in other books that will unlock your ability to hear God's voice more clearly, but the truth is that God has already unlocked your ability to hear God when Jesus sent the Holy Spirit to live inside you. The only thing stopping you and me from hearing God's voice to our thoughts is our doubt and unbelief.

Matthew 9:29 (KJV) says, *"According to your faith be it unto you."*

This means that if you believe you *can* hear God, then you *will* hear God. If you don't believe that you can hear God, then you *won't* hear God. So, again, what is the only thing stopping you from hearing God's voice and operating in the gifts of the Spirit?

3. Knowing the power of childlike faith is what will allow you to fully understand and apply this next verse—1 Peter 4:11.

Verse: (Pray it as you say it 10 times or more to memorize it.)

"If anyone speaks, he should do it as one speaking the very words of God."
1 Peter 4:11

What is the full meaning of this verse to you?

How could this kind of "Godfidence" change your life and the lives of those around you?

Once you know that God wants to simply flow through your mouth to His world, then everything changes. You will no longer fear messing up or looking stupid. You will simply open your mouth and let God fill it, expecting Him to do what only He can do!

Response:

Post these two verses in a prominent place in your home, and make them a prominent part of your life. Every time you go to the grocery, work, school, the gym or the coffee shop, remind yourself that you can hear God's voice. Then step out in confidence and be a set of humble lips through which God can speak!

Section 2—Satan Wants You to Stay in the Truck

Read:

No More No pp. 77-84 (Chapter 5—Step Out in Confidence)

Verse:

"You belong to your father, the devil, and you want to carry out your father's desires. He was a murderer from the beginning, not holding to the truth, for there is no truth in him. When he lies, he speaks his native language, for he is a liar and the father of lies."

John 8:44

1. When you are in a battle it's important to know the tactics of your enemy. Fortunately for us, the only tactics the devil has against us are his lies. He is a liar and the father of lies.

   What do you think that means?

   Every lie that has ever been told was birthed from the devil and is daily propagated by the devil and his demons. If he can get you to believe his lies, he can keep you from fighting your spiritual battles with the weapons God provided for you, and he can get you to carry out his desires rather than God's.

2. Every time you believe the devil's lies—that you can't hear God's voice, that you aren't spiritual enough to deliver gifts of healing, miracles and words from God's heart, that you can't walk in supernatural love, kindness and patience—then you are carrying out the desires of the devil.

   Pause a moment and think about that. How does that make you feel?

3. Once you know that God has provided gifts for you to deliver, the devil will have his demons working relentlessly to lie to you in order to stop you from getting out of your delivery truck. Why? Because you have now become a threat to the kingdom of darkness and deception.

What lies have you been battling the past few weeks as you have been making a point to let God highlight people with His love and pray for them?

How are you learning to overcome and ignore those lies?

4. Read the five stories on pp. 79-84 of *No More No* and identify the lies, fears and doubts that the enemy spoke to me or might have spoken to me in each of those encounters to keep me from speaking. Then identify the truth that counters each lie.

"Handcuffed" (p. 79)

"Mascara" (pp. 79-80)

"The Love of a Mother" (pp. 80-82)

"Delayed Obedience" (pp. 82-83)

"The Preacher" (pp.83-84)

Section 3—Everyone Misses It at Times

Read:

No More No pp. 84-88 (Chapter 5—Step Out in Confidence)

Verse:

"When Peter came to Antioch, I opposed him to his face, because he was clearly in the wrong"

Galatians 2:11

1. Although Peter had done amazing miracles and been used mightily by God, he still messed up and missed it at times. Paul had to correct Peter for becoming legalistic and hypocritical in trying to force Gentiles to follow Jewish laws rather than teaching salvation by grace alone.

   I gave several other examples in *No More No* of Peter and Paul messing up along with a few modern-day men of God. What would have happened to the church in the past, and what would happen now, if men and women threw in the towel and quit trying to follow God's leading every time they didn't hear God's voice accurately or didn't walk in perfect love or perfect theology?

2. What will happen if you throw in the towel every time you don't see a healing or are wrong when you try to hear a word of knowledge for someone?

   How many people will you reach with the love of Jesus if you refuse to take risks and keep trying?

3. Todd White and Dan Mohler are great examples of pushing forward even when you miss a word or don't see someone healed. Todd prayed for over 1,000 people for healing before he began to see people healed. Now he sees people healed regularly and you can watch him and Dan share their amazing stories on YouTube.

Go to YouTube right now and pull up "Todd White Healing" and watch a short story just for fun. The only reason those stories are happening is because he doesn't give up every time he messes up or every time someone is mean to him.

The only reason Todd and Dan are seeing such incredible words given, healings taking place and countless people saved is because they refuse to give up. The only reason I am finally seeing more healings and more accurate words is because I refuse to give up.

4. I love the story "Dane's Persistence" (pp.87-88 in *No More No*). As you read it, count how many times Dane (my son) missed words of knowledge yet continued to persist in listening for God's voice so that he could bless that precious couple for the Lord.

   How many times did he mess up, but not give up?

5. If Dane can push forward relentlessly in order to connect His Jesus with his world, then you can too. There is nothing special or different about Dane, Todd, Dan, me or anyone else who lives this lifestyle.

   We just refuse to give up and you can too!

Response:

Take some time to talk with the Father about your resolve to live a lifestyle of never giving up no matter what lies, fears, doubts, attacks or obstacles come your way. Write a prayer to Him:

Imagine how wonderful it will be to stand before God in heaven one day and say to Him, "I didn't always get it right, but I never gave up! You were worth every sacrifice—and the people you love passionately were worth every sacrifice!"

Section 4—Let the Conversations Flow

Read:

No More No pp. 129-137 (First half of Chapter 8—Still Marching)

1. As you read the stories below, write down how each conversation got started and the first sentence or two of each encounter.

   "Divine Leading" (pp. 129-131)

   "Victorious Victor" (pp. 131-132)

   "Drips from Heaven" (pp. 132-134)

   "God's Rapper" (pp. 135-137)

2. Each encounter took a leap of faith. Did God come through for me each time or did He leave me in the lurch? Can you write down an example or two from these stories, or your own stories, of when God came through for me or you?

God is always faithful to catch us when we leap. Trust Him!

3. Some people comment that they don't know what to say once they get started in an encounter. It is perfectly normal to start out with shorter conversations until you get more comfortable talking about Jesus and your testimony.

At what point do you sometimes get hung up or struggle with how to proceed?

If you do struggle, have you now learned some tips to keep the conversation going? (Once I share my word or impression or ask someone if they need prayer, I like to ask them, "What is your spiritual background?" or "Do you have a relationship with the Lord, yet?")

Don't expect your conversations to necessarily flow as easily as mine did in these stories. Remember, I was saying *yes* to God's promptings for at least 2½ years before these stories in this chapter took place. (And I talked with people about Jesus for many years before that.) Start where you are at and let God grow you. God is still growing me!

Chapter Highlights: (*No More No* p. 89)

Read the Chapter Highlights and Application for review and inspiration.

Week 5: Group Wrap-Up

Group Session #6

- Will someone please open us in prayer?

- [Discuss past or upcoming outreaches as a group.]

- Last week's "You Can Do It":
    - ❖ How did it go when you asked God to highlight at least two people with His love last week?
    - ❖ What are some of your stories?
    - ❖ What were your challenges, and how can we pray for you as you choose to step out in love?

- Next week's "You Can Do It":
    - ❖ Continue to pray silently for people you pass and interact with, and be intentional to talk with strangers, making them feel important and loved.
    - ❖ This week again ask God to highlight at least two strangers with His love. Express God's heart, taking risks to listen for God's voice for them, and then pray for them.
    - ❖ Also ask at least two people that you interact with if they have any prayer needs, and pray right then. This could be someone at your door, a cashier, a waitress, a co-worker, etc.

- Section 1 Discussion: You Can Hear God
    - ❖ Let's read out loud from pages 76-77 in *No More No* under "You Can Hear God," and discuss Julie's comments and the truths of John 8:47 and 1 Peter 4:11.
    - ❖ Read Matthew 9:29.
    - ❖ What does this verse mean?
    - ❖ Why could understanding this truth totally revolutionize your life?

- Section 2 Discussion: Satan Wants You to Stay in the Truck
    - ❖ Read John 8:44.
    - ❖ Is the devil capable of anything but lies?
    - ❖ What is the goal of the devil's lies when it comes to us working for God's Parcel Service?
    - ❖ If we believe and act on the devil's lies rather than God's truth, who is it we are working for and serving?

❖ How does that make you feel to know that you are always serving either God or the enemy?

❖ Discuss some of the fears, doubts and lies that the devil might have attacked Julie with in the stories listed in Section 2. (See p. 73 in this study guide.)

• Section 3 Discussion: Everyone Misses It at Times

❖ Read Galatians 2:11.

❖ Paul had to rebuke Peter for stepping back into legalism. What if Peter, as a result, felt unworthy and embarrassed, so he threw in the towel, no longer sharing the Good News of Jesus with his world?

❖ You will listen for words of knowledge for people and miss it, and you will pray for people for healing and they won't be healed. The devil wants you to give up and throw in the towel, but what does God want you to do?

❖ How many of you watched a video clip of Todd White with Lifestyle Christianity? What did you think?

❖ The key he discovered is to never give up even when you mess up. God loves your heart and your efforts!

❖ In the story entitled "Dane's Persistence" how many times did Dane hear an incorrect word? What did he do even though he kept missing it with words of knowledge? What happened as a result?

❖ Remember the only difference between those who walk in the power of God and those who don't is that one perseveres and the other gives up.

• Section 4 Discussion: Let the Conversations Flow

❖ Discuss a few of your observations of how God started conversations in Julie's stories. (See p. 76 of this study guide.)

❖ Do you struggle in knowing what to say once you get started in an encounter with someone?

❖ Asking people about their spiritual background or if they have a relationship with the Lord yet will keep the conversation going. Share any tips or ideas that help you keep talking as you let the Holy Spirit flow through you.

❖ Don't forget the Conversation Starters on pp. 145-146.

• Let's pray

Before we practice hearing from God, remember to:
1. Silence the devil's lies.
2. Speak God's truth.
3. Expect God to be BIG through you.

Practice in a Safe Place:

#1: Everyone stand in one spread-out circle, facing outward with your backs to each other and your eyes closed, if necessary, in order to not see the people beside you. I will also be a part of the circle. When I discreetly tap you on the shoulder from behind, you will go to the middle of the circle and stand there quietly, not letting anyone know who you are. Then the rest of the group will share pictures and words that they have for the person in the middle. (The person in the middle may want to turn on his or her phone recorder before they begin.)

Once three or four people have shared words and pictures, we will all turn around and see who was in the middle. Then that person will share what the words meant to him or her. Be gentle and encouraging in your evaluations, realizing that some of the words might not make sense right now, but could make sense later.

We will continue to do this as long as we have time.

#2: If someone is in need of prayer ministry, raise your hand and then we'll have one or two other people gather around you to pray and hear God's heart of love and wisdom.

Week 6:

Keep it Fun and Stress Free

Week 6: Keep it Fun and Stress Free
Quick Version

Prayer:

Thank you that walking with you, Jesus, is such fun!

You Can Do It: (Don't forget to write or audio-record your encounters.)

Pray silently for everyone you pass or interact with all week.

Chit-chat with strangers to let them know they are seen and important.

Tell at least two strangers that God highlighted them with His love, and then express words from God's heart. Take risks because people are worth it! Then offer to pray, and pray right then.

Pray with at least two strangers whom God has you interact with, (cashier, waiter, waitress, sales person, etc.) and ask God to carry the conversation beyond just prayer.

Reading:

No More No pp. 91-104 (Chapter 6—Keep it Fun and Stress Free)

Reading time: 15 minutes

Notes, comments or questions from your reading, and ideas for applying it to your life:

Week 6: Keep it Fun and Stress Free
Going Deeper

Prayer:

Thank you that walking with you, Jesus, is such fun!

You Can Do It: (Don't forget to write or audio-record your encounters.)

Pray silently for everyone you pass or interact with all week.

Chit-chat with strangers to let them know they are seen and important.

Tell at least two strangers that God highlighted them with His love, and then express words from God's heart. Take risks because people are worth it! Then offer to pray, and pray right then.

Pray with at least two strangers whom God has you interact with, (cashier, waiter, waitress, sales person, etc.) and ask God to carry the conversation beyond just prayer.

Section 1—Tips 1 through 5

Read:

No More No pp. 91-93 (Chapter 6—Keep it Fun and Stress Free)

Directions:

Write each of the 5 tips and then write the highlights of each of those tips. If you can, write a personal story of how you have been able to apply, or need to apply, those principles in your own life.

Tip #1: _____

Tip #2: _____

Tip #3: _____

Tip #4: _____

Tip #5: _____

Section 2—Tips 6 through 11

Read:

No More No pp. 93-96 (Chapter 6—Keep it Fun and Stress Free)

Directions:

Write each of the 6 tips and then write the highlights of each of those tips. If you can, write a personal story of how you have been able to apply, or need to apply, those principles in your own life.

Tip #6: _____

Tip #7: _____

Tip #8: _____

Tip #9: _____

Tip #10: _____

Tip #11: _____

Section 3—Tips 12 through 17

Read:

No More No pp. 96-100 (Chapter 6—Keep it Fun and Stress Free)

Directions:

Write each of the 6 tips and then write the highlights of each of those tips. If you can, write a personal story of how you have been able to apply, or need to apply, those principles in your own life.

Tip #12: _____

Tip #13: _____

Tip #14: _____

Tip #15: _____

Tip #16: _____

Tip #17: _____

Section 4—Tips 18 through 23

Read:

No More No pp. 100-103 (Chapter 6—Keep it Fun and Stress Free)

Chapter Highlights and Application pp. 103-104

Directions:

Write each of the 6 tips and then write the highlights of each of those tips. If you can, write a personal story of how you have been able to apply, or need to apply, those principles in your own life.

Tip #18: _____

Tip #19: _____

Tip #20: _____

Tip #21: _____

Tip #22: _____

Tip #23: _____

Week 6: Group Wrap-Up and Outreach

Group Session #7—Outreach

- Let's pray, silencing fear of man and every lie of the devil that would stop us from doing the works Jesus promised we would do.

- Before the outreach, we are going to take 10 minutes and have each of you read a tip from this chapter and share a 20-second synopsis of the tip, rotating through the group until we have quickly covered all 23 tips. Then we are going to head out to love on people in groups of two for about an hour. We will then return to share our stories and pray for the people God highlighted or led us to.

- [Have everyone read a tip and then give a 20-second synopsis. See pp. 91-103 in *No More No* or pp. 84-91 in this study guide.]

OUTREACH:

- Let's divide into groups of 2 with the more confident people going with the less confident. Ask the Holy Spirit to direct your heart as to where to go. Don't overthink it. Just go to wherever pops into your head. It can be nearby stores, a park or a neighborhood. (You can also go in groups of 4 and break up into groups of 2 once you arrive if the store or location is large enough for two groups.)

- Before we go, let's read the suggestions for what we can do.

  Once you arrive you can:
  - ❖ **Tell someone God highlighted them** with His love and express God's words of love for them. For example, "When I saw you, the Lord highlighted you with His love...."

  - ❖ Tell someone that you are out praying God's blessings for people, and **ask if they have any prayer needs**, and then pray with them. For example, "We are out praying for people this evening. Do you have any prayer needs? Is there anything going on with your health, your family or some other issue?"

  - ❖ **Ask God to give you a word for someone**, and then express that word along with other things God speaks to your thoughts. For example, "We are Christians and we are learning how to hear God's voice, not only for us but for other people. Do you have a family member who is struggling with finances? Depression? (Etc.)"

❖ **Pray for someone who you sense has health issues or you can see has health issues.** After you pray for them, have the person test it out, expecting God to heal them. (To make them not feel pressured to say they are better when they might not be, say something like, "If you can feel your symptoms right now, did you notice anything different or is it the same?" or "What was your pain level when we started? Is it the same or has it gotten better?" Pray again if needed.)

❖ **Most of all have fun!** Share the love the Father has showered upon you! Being nervous is just the enemy trying to stop you, so ignore him and go for it.

IF THEY RECEIVE JESUS' FORGIVENESS: If you share with someone how to be saved and they pray to receive Jesus' forgiveness, make sure to get their contact information and give them yours. If they don't want to pray right there, tell them how to receive Christ once they get home.

The bottom line is, "Jesus forgive me and send your Spirit, the Holy Spirit, to live inside me so that we can do life together with You now leading the way."

AFTER THE OUTREACH:
• [When everyone comes back after the outreach, have them share a few highlights from their stories and then pray for the people that were ministered to. Discuss any challenges that you faced.]

Week 7:

Fall in Love with Jesus

Week 7: Fall in Love with Jesus
Quick Version

Prayer:

Open my eyes to the wonders of your love, Jesus!

You Can Do It: (Don't forget to write or audio-record your encounters.)

Pick 3 ways you want to boldly express God's heart this week:

1.

2.

3.

Reading:

No More No pp. 165-184 (Chapter 10—Fall in Love with Jesus)

No More No pp. 137-147 (Second half of Chapter 8—Still Marching)

Reading time for both sections: 24 minutes and 11 minutes

Notes, comments or questions from your reading, and ideas for applying it to your life:

Week 7: Fall in Love with Jesus
Going Deeper

Prayer:

Open my eyes to the wonders of your love, Jesus!

You Can Do It: (Don't forget to write or audio-record your encounters.)

Pick 3 ways you want to boldly express God's heart this week:

1.

2.

3.

Section 1—The Benefits of Falling in Love with Jesus

Read:

No More No pp. 165-173 (Chapter 10—Fall in Love with Jesus)

Verse: (Pray it as you say it 8 times in order to memorize it.)

"Love the Lord your God with all your heart and with all your soul and with all your mind and with all your strength."

Mark 12:30

1. This verse is the most important truth in this book and in the Bible. What does it mean to you?

If you want to say *yes* to God...fall in love with Jesus!
If you want to get victory over sin...fall in love with Jesus!
If you want to have joy in the midst of pain...fall in love with Jesus!
If you want revelation and insight...fall in love with Jesus!
If you want the gifts of the Spirit to flow...fall in love with Jesus!

What are a few stories of victory where your growing love relationship with Jesus has transformed your life?

2. Read Hebrews 12:1-2. You have the incredible privilege of running your race with Jesus because the Holy Spirit (God's Spirit, the Spirit of Jesus) lives in you. What are some things you may still need to "throw off" that are hindering your race, and how can you better fix your eyes on Jesus?

I still battle fixing my eyes on snacks and Hallmark videos on YouTube in the evenings. It may sound small, but it is often a big frustration for me. I need to quit believing the lie that I will be happier "chewing and viewing," and I need to follow Jesus' lead. Ha!

3. 1 Corinthians 2:9-10 says, *"'No eye has seen, no ear has heard, no mind has conceived what God has prepared for those who love him'—but God has revealed it to us by his Spirit."* Ask the Holy Spirit to reveal to you the incredible things He has prepared for your life if you simply fall in love with Jesus. What will change and what will you be able to do?

Section 2—Practical Ideas for Intimacy (Part 1)

Read:

No More No pp. 173-178 (Chapter 10—Fall in Love with Jesus)

Directions:

Write down each of the ideas for intimacy with Jesus, and then give a synopsis of the important points in your own words, along with any scriptures given. Add any of your own thoughts as well!

#1: _____

#2: _____

#3: _____

#4: _____

#5: _____

#6: _____

#7: _____

Section 3—Practical Ideas for Intimacy (Part 2)

Read:

No More No pp. 178-183 (Chapter 10—Fall in Love with Jesus)

Directions:

Write down each of the ideas for intimacy with Jesus, and then give a synopsis of the important points in your own words, along with any scriptures given. Add any of your own thoughts as well!

#8: _____

#9: _____

#10: _____

#11: _____

#12: _____

#13: _____

#14: _____

Section 4—Follow the Way of Love

Read:

No More No pp. 137-147 (Second half of Chapter 8—Still Marching)

Verse: (Pray it as you say it 5 times.)

"Follow the way of love and eagerly desire spiritual gifts, especially the gift of prophecy."

1 Corinthians 14:1

For each of the stories, make notes of the "way of love" that was taken and the spiritual gifts that were given—words of knowledge, wisdom or prophecy, an act of kindness, an offer to pray, words of encouragement, words of love or sharing the Good News of salvation.

"Words for Children, a Veteran and Discounted Apples" (pp. 137-139)

"How's Your Heart?" (p. 140)

"Gifts of Love on the Phone" (pp.140-142)

"God's Not Dead" (pp. 142-145)

"Sweet Hannah" (pp. 146-147)

Chapter Highlights: (_No More No_ pp. 183-184)

Read the Chapter Highlights and Application for review and inspiration.

Week 7: Group Wrap-Up

Group Session #8 [Have a pen and sheet of paper for each person.]

- Let's pray.

- [Discuss past or upcoming outreaches as a group.]

- Last week's "You Can Do It":
    - ❖ What 3 ways to express God's love did you choose and what stories do you have?
    - ❖ Are you ignoring the lies and fears of the enemy, and if so, what is happening as a result?
    - ❖ If fear is stopping you, how can we help you ignore the fear and go for it?

- Next week's "You Can Do It":
    - ❖ Rather than setting up goals for yourself, now it's time to let Jesus lead you moment by moment.
    - ❖ Wherever you go, be in tune to people that He highlights, people you bump into who you can offer to pray for and pictures and impressions He gives you in your spirit.

- Section 1 Discussion: The Benefits of Falling in Love with Jesus
    - ❖ Read Mark 12:30.
    - ❖ In what ways will your life be transformed as you fall in love with Jesus?
    - ❖ What are your stories of victory where your growing love relationship with Jesus is transforming your life? (See the top of p. 99 in this study guide.)
    - ❖ Read Hebrews 12:1-2.
    - ❖ What are some things that may be hindering your race and your ability to fix your eyes on Jesus?
    - ❖ Read 1 Corinthians 2:9-10.
    - ❖ What incredible things has the Holy Spirit prepared for you as you simply fall in love with Jesus? (Also on p. 99.)

- Section 2 and 3 Discussion: Practical Ideas for Intimacy (Parts 1 & 2)
    - ❖ Let's read through each of the 14 Practical Ideas for Intimacy, discussing the highlights and anything that especially stood out to you. (See pp. 173-183 in *No More No* or pp. 100-103 in this study guide.)

106

❖ What are 2 or 3 ideas that you want to implement this week and in the future?

- Section 4 Discussion: Follow the Way of Love
  - ❖ Read 1 Corinthians 14:1.
  - ❖ What is the way of love—the GPS journey of love—that you feel God is calling you to? What is He asking of you?
  - ❖ Do you have any comments about the God Encounter stories from the second half of Chapter 8—Still Marching? (See pp. 137-147 in *No More No* or pp. 104-105 in this study guide.)

- Let's pray.

Before we practice hearing from God, remember to:
  1. Silence the devil's lies.
  2. Speak God's truth.
  3. Expect God to be BIG through you.

Practice in a Safe Place:

#1: Let's all sit in a circle and everyone will get a piece of paper and a pen. Ask the Holy Spirit to give you a prophetic picture and the meaning of the picture that will strengthen, encourage or comfort someone in our group. (You won't know who it is for, but trust God to give you the right picture and word.) We will take 3 to 5 minutes to write down the description of the picture we see in our mind's eye (or draw it if possible) and the meaning of the picture. Once we are done, I will gather the papers up and randomly pass them out to everyone in the circle, trusting God will give the right one to each person. (If you get your own paper, then the word must be for you.) Then we will take turns reading out loud what we each received, discussing it if you would like. The person who wrote the word can reveal themselves or keep it a secret. It is up to them.

#2: If someone is in need of prayer ministry, raise your hand and then we'll have one or two other people gather around you to pray and hear God's heart of love and wisdom.

Week 8:

Fall in Love with People

Week 8: Fall in Love with People
Quick Version

Prayer:

Help me fall in love with the people you love passionately!

You Can Do It: (Don't forget to write or audio-record your encounters.)

Now it's time to let Jesus lead you moment by moment.

Be in tune to God's highlights, be aware of the people you can pray with, and constantly ask for pictures, words and impressions. Expect God to work through you and He will!

Reading:

No More No pp. 185-199 (Chapter 11—Fall in Love with People)

No More No pp. 149-161 (Chapter 9—Other Radicals I Know)

Reading time for both sections: 20 minutes and 16 minutes

Notes, comments or questions from your reading, and ideas for applying it to your life:

Week 8: Fall in Love with People
Going Deeper

Prayer:

Help me fall in love with the people you love passionately!

You Can Do It: (Don't forget to write or audio-record your encounters.)

Now it's time to let Jesus lead you moment by moment.

Be in tune to God's highlights, be aware of the people you can pray with, and constantly ask for pictures, words and impressions. Expect God to work through you and He will!

Section 1—How to Fall in Love with People

Read:

No More No pp. 185-189 (Chapter 11—Fall in Love with People)

Verse: (Pray it as you say it 5 times.)

"I urge, then, first of all, that requests, prayers, intercession and thanksgiving be made for everyone—"

1 Timothy 2:1

1. When the Lord made it clear to me that the "everyone" we are supposed to pray for in 1 Timothy 2:1 is truly "everyone," my world was transformed. As I began praying silently for everyone I passed at the grocery store, while driving and wherever I went, God's love for people began to explode in my heart. How could I not tell these incredible people I prayed for every day that God loves them passionately and wants to spend now and eternity with them?

   Since you have been praying silently for people from the beginning of this study, what changes have you seen in your heart?

2. On page 186 in *No More No* I wrote: "Amazingly, this simple act of praying God's love and truth on everyone around me was dissolving

112

my fears. My love *for* people became greater than my fear *of* people. My concern for *them* became greater than my concern for *me*."

Have you found this to be true? Can you explain?

Have you seen a shift in your attitude toward people when they cut you off in traffic, speak rudely to you or intentionally hurt you? Can you give an example?

Why is it hard to be mad at the very people you are constantly praying blessings upon?

3. Proverbs 14:22 says, *"Those who plan what is good find love and faithfulness."*

Think of a couple people in your life for whom you realize your love needs to grow. Then list 2 or 3 practical ideas of ways you can "plan what is good" and do acts of kindness as you choose to *do love* even when you don't *feel love*.

List 2 or 3 acts of love that you can begin doing for strangers. (Feel free to use ideas from pages 188-189 of *No More No*.)

Section 2—Shyness is Not of God

Read:

No More No pp. 189-191 (Chapter 11—Fall in Love with People)

Verse: (Pray it as you say it 5 times.)

"All of you, clothe yourselves with humility toward one another, because, 'God opposes the proud but gives grace to the humble.'"

1 Peter 5:5b

1. What is the root of pride and why does God oppose it?

2. Why are shyness and not speaking when God prompts you both a form of pride?

3. List the 4 steps to finding freedom from shyness (p. 190 in *No More No*), and add your personal thoughts or scriptures to each of those points:

4. Proverbs 16:24 says, *"Pleasant words are a honeycomb, sweet to the soul and healing to the bones."* Why is this true?

As you have more intentionally chatted with people and made them feel important and seen, how has it affected you and them?

List practical ideas and conversation starters that you can use to continue to speak "pleasant words" and heal hearts wherever you go: (Page 191 in *No More No* has a few ideas to get you started.)

Section 3—Express God's Love

Read:

No More No pp. 192-198 (Chapter 11—Fall in Love with People)

Verse: (Pray it as you say it 5 times.)

"I have loved you with an everlasting love; I have drawn you with loving-kindness.'"

Jeremiah 31:3

1. If fear and doubt are keeping you from listening for God's voice and operating in His healing power, then listen for God's love and start there. Work with the Holy Spirit to draw people to God's heart with words of His loving-kindness. When God highlights someone to you, open your mouth by faith and begin speaking words of love and truth over them.

   List the 4 areas of God's love mentioned on page 193 of *No More No* (along with some of the verses mentioned) and then add other verses you find that speak about the depth of God's love for people:

2. Read Romans 8:38-39 and ask God to sink it deep into your heart that even if someone rejects Jesus' forgiveness and spends eternity in hell outside the influence and blessing of God's love, God will still feel intense love for them for eternity. (See pages 194-195 of *No More No*.)

In light of this truth, ask yourself, "How much do I truly love God and care about His heart? Do I care that His heart will ache for eternity over each person who rejects Him?"

"How much do I truly love people? Do I care that without receiving Jesus' forgiveness, they will spend eternity in eternal torment apart from any influence or effect of God's love?

3. Read Matthew 16:24 and list specific ways God is asking you to deny yourself, take up your cross and follow Him.

4. Can you think of people in your life who you are not loving enough because you aren't tuning into God's voice or you aren't reaching out to them when the Spirit prompts you? Write down a few ideas God gives you for loving them.

Write Your Prayer of Turning and Surrender:

Section 4—Other Radicals I Know

Read:

No More No pp. 149-161 (Chapter 9—Other Radicals I Know)

This fun chapter tells other people's stories of saying *yes* to God's promptings. If you have the time and umph, feel free to write down any thoughts or tips from each of the stories. (Or just enjoy the stories and be inspired!)

"Cussed Out in Church" by Barbara Shippy (pp. 149-152)

"Healing in Sporting Goods" by Karis Johnston (pp. 152-154)

"Illogical Obedience" by Camille Collie (pp.154-155)

"Too Much Pain to Live" by Richelle Beltrand (pp. 156-157)

"Concern in Her Eyes" by Stuart Gurnea (pp. 157-158)

"Skateboarder Restored" by Dane Earl (pp. 158-161)

Chapter Highlights: (*No More No* pp. 198-199)

Read the Chapter Highlights and Application for review and inspiration.

Week 8: Group Wrap-Up

Group Session #9

- Will someone please open us in prayer?

- [Discuss any business.]

- Last week's "You Can Do It":
  - ❖ How did it go as you let Jesus lead you moment by moment last week?
  - ❖ Do you have any stories, concerns or victories?

- Next week's "You Can Do It":
  - ❖ Once again allow the Holy Spirit to lead you wherever you go.
  - ❖ Expect God to speak, love and heal through you in every setting you walk into. The promptings and highlights will be very faint, and the enemy will try to talk you out of them, but jump right in each time and see what God does. Even if you start talking and it wasn't necessarily a prompting from the Holy Spirit, God will show up and bless the person and bless you—so it is a win-win situation.

- Section 1 Discussion: How to Fall in Love with People
  - ❖ Read 1 Timothy 2:1.
  - ❖ Who are we supposed to pray for?
  - ❖ How has praying silently for people you pass affected:
    - ▪ The love you feel for people?
    - ▪ The love you feel for Jesus?
    - ▪ Your patience while driving?
    - ▪ Your fear of man?
  - ❖ Read Proverbs 14:22b.
  - ❖ In order to fall in love with people, we often have to *do* love until we *feel* love. Do you have a story of this happening in any of your relationships with family or friends?
  - ❖ What are a few practical ways we can *do* love until we *feel* love?

- Section 2 Discussion: Shyness is Not of God
  - ❖ Read 1 Peter 5:5b.

❖ Why does God oppose the proud and give grace to the humble?

❖ Why is shyness a form of pride?

❖ Why is not saying *yes* to God's promptings a form of pride?

❖ What are the 4 steps to finding freedom from shyness (found on p. 190 of *No More No*)? Let's discuss them.

❖ Read Proverbs 16:24.

❖ As you have made it a priority to chat with people and make them feel important and seen, have you found Proverbs 16:24 to be true?

❖ Did chatting with people decrease your shyness and fear of people?

- Section 3 Discussion: Express God's Love

  ❖ Read Jeremiah 31:3.

  ❖ Why are people drawn to God?

  ❖ If fear and doubt are keeping you from listening for God's voice, then listen for God's love and start there. Work with the Holy Spirit to draw people to God's heart with words of His loving-kindness.

  ❖ Let's discuss the 4 areas of God's love we can express that are mentioned on page 193 of *No More No*.

  ❖ Read Romans 8:38-39.

  ❖ This passage says that God will love us for eternity, which means He will love us whether we spend eternity in heaven or hell. God will grieve over every single person who spends eternity suffering apart from Him.

  ❖ Does this truth affect your willingness to lay down your life for others and do everything God asks you to do every day?

  ❖ Let's pray right now and ask God to break our hearts for what breaks His. [Play worship music if available and feel free to kneel.]

- Section 4 Discussion: Other Radicals I Know

  [You may want to skip the discussion of these stories (or discuss very briefly after praying) so that you can spend more time in prayer.]

Before we practice hearing from God, remember to:
1. Silence the devil's lies.
2. Speak God's truth.
3. Expect God to be BIG through you.

Practice in a Safe Place: [A blindfold would be helpful.]

#1: Let's all stand in a tight circle facing each other. I will pick one person at a time to stand in the middle blindfolded or with their eyes closed. We will gently spin the person around and then have them point to someone in the circle. They won't know who they are pointing to, so they will ask the Holy Spirit to give them His words for that person and then they will step out by faith and take whatever risk they are comfortable with.

They might express:
- God's heart of love for that person.
- Something the Lord loves about them.
- Something coming up in their future.
- A word of knowledge that only they would know.
- A Bible verse that the Holy Spirit brings to mind for them.

They will then take off the mask, or open their eyes, and see who received the prophetic word. The person who did receive the word, if they are comfortable, can share what the word meant to them. (Remember that some words from the Lord may not make sense until later, so you may have to simply say you aren't yet sure what it means.) Make sure to encourage the person who gave you the word and took a risk to hear God's voice for you!

We will keep doing this as long as we have time. If someone points to a person in the circle who has already received a word, I may move someone else from the circle to their place before the person starts to prophesy over them so that more people can receive words and be blessed.

#2: If someone is in need of prayer ministry, raise your hand and then we'll have one or two other people gather around you to pray and hear God's heart of love and wisdom.

Week 9:

Know Who You Are and Whose You Are

Week 9: Know Who You Are and Whose You Are
Quick Version

Prayer:

Thank you, Holy Spirit, for making me a superhero!

You Can Do It: (Don't forget to write or audio-record your encounters.)

Once again allow the Holy Spirit to lead you wherever you go.

Expect God to speak, love and heal through you in every setting you walk into. The promptings and highlights will be very faint, and the enemy will try to talk you out of them, but jump right in each time and see what God does. Even if you start talking and it wasn't necessarily a prompting from the Holy Spirit, God will show up and bless the person and bless you—so it's a win-win situation!

Reading:

No More No pp. 201-216 (Chapter 12—Know Who You Are and Whose You Are)

No More No pp. 217-222 (You Can Do It!)

Reading time for both sections: 20 minutes and 8 minutes

Notes, comments or questions from your reading, and ideas for applying it to your life:

Week 9: Know Who You Are and Whose You Are
Going Deeper

Prayer:

Thank you, Holy Spirit, for making me a superhero!

You Can Do It: (Don't forget to write or audio-record your encounters.)

Once again allow the Holy Spirit to lead you wherever you go.

Expect God to speak, love and heal through you in every setting you walk into. The promptings and highlights will be very faint, and the enemy will try to talk you out of them, but jump right in each time and see what God does. Even if you start talking and it wasn't necessarily a prompting from the Holy Spirit, God will show up and bless the person and bless you—so it's a win-win situation!

Section 1—Power Up Your Super Suit

Read:

No More No pp. 201-204 (Chapter 12—Know Who You Are and Whose You Are)

Verse: (Pray it as you say it 5 times.)

"You are all sons of God through faith in Christ Jesus, for all of you who were baptized into Christ have clothed yourselves with Christ"

Galatians 3:26-27

1. As soon as you believe in Jesus as your Savior and Lord, inviting the Holy Spirit to baptize you in His love and power, you become a superhero and a Parcel Wonder because you are clothed in Christ. If it helps, picture yourself every day inside a Jesus costume, but this costume comes fully loaded, similar to the Iron Man suit!

   Read the following scriptures, making notes of just how powerful your Super Suit is and what it has equipped you to do:

   Ephesians 1:18-22

126

Matthew 10:7-8

Acts 1:8

Acts 4:31

Mark 11:23-24

Philippians 4:13

2. Read John 8:44. What is the main weapon the devil uses to keep you from powering up your Super Suit and doing the works of Jesus every day?

What lies does the devil use against you, and what can you do to defeat his lies, attacks and hindrances?

Never forget that you are not just a conqueror, but more than a conqueror through Jesus (Romans 8:37). You are truly a superhero, so power-up that Super Suit and defeat the works of darkness!

Section 2—Discover the Real You

Read:

No More No pp. 204-210 (Chapter 12—Know Who You Are and Whose You Are)

Verse: (Pray it as you say it 5 times.)

"Therefore, if anyone is in Christ, he is a new creation; the old has gone, the new has come!"

2 Corinthians 5:17

1. Thanks to Jesus and all He suffered, you have the privilege of becoming a new creation once you are in Christ—once you are in your Super Suit. It is vital, then, that you discover what a new creation looks like so that you can fulfill the purposes God has for you—the real you.

   Knowing that you are completely forgiven and not under any condemnation is first and foremost in discovering the real you. (See Romans 8:1.)

   List areas where the enemy or your flesh have made you feel condemned. How did that affect your attitude and actions? Did you have much impact in the Kingdom or did you feel too unworthy to be God's hands, voice and feet on the earth?

   Make sure to read this section on pages 206-209 in *No More No* until the truth that you are 100% forgiven goes past your head into your heart. Remember, God's Spirit couldn't live inside you if your sins weren't truly washed whiter than snow. What do the verses below say and mean?

   Isaiah 1:18

   John 1:29

128

2 Corinthians 5:21

1 John 3:9

Your soul and your mind are daily being renewed and transformed, but your spirit is a new creation and sin free. When you know the Father loves you and does not condemn you, your desire to please, honor and love Him with your actions and obedience will grow exponentially. Can you give an example of this in your life?

2. I have often mentioned the fact that God loves you passionately, but if that truth isn't yours, go after it with every fiber of your being. You absolutely must know that you are the apple of God's eye—His treasure and His delight. Look up verses on God's love for you and plaster them all around your house, car and workplace. Ask the Holy Spirit to break off the lies of the enemy and reveal His heart of love for you. God's love truly changes everything!

3. One of my greatest griefs is when people blame the sin, sickness, death and attacks of the enemy on our loving, incredible, perfect Father. It makes me weep. Explain how the following factors can affect us negatively, proving that God is not the culprit:

Free will

Our fallen world

Lack of faith for the supernatural

Section 3—Take Back Your Authority

Read:

No More No pp. 211-215 (Chapter 12—Know Who You Are and Whose You Are)

Verse: (Pray it as you say it 5 times.)

"The heaven, even the heavens, are the LORD's: but the earth hath he given to the children of men."

Psalm 115:16 (KJV)

1. Not understanding the authority that God has given us on the earth is another reason for much of the suffering and pain mankind experiences needlessly. God has given us as "the children of men" authority. But ever since the fall of Adam and Eve, the enemy has been robbing us of our authority—by convincing us that we don't have any.

   Jesus' mission was to destroy the works of the devil and the lies that stripped us of our inheritance, rights and authority on the earth. What are the incredible truths found in the following scriptures?

   Matthew 8:25-27

   Matthew 10:1

   Matthew 16:19

   Matthew 28:18-20

   Luke 10:19

John 14:12

You will have tribulations and trials on the earth (John 16:33) because you are daily dealing with people (yourself included) who have free will to choose love and be a blessing or to choose evil and cause harm. But that doesn't negate the areas where you do have power and authority. You have power and authority over sickness, disease, demons, animals, bugs, plants, the weather and mountains!

Ask the Holy Spirit to open your eyes and give you childlike faith to believe that if Jesus said it, then that settles it. Then step out by faith and use your power and authority to speak to your mountains in Jesus' name!

Write out a declaration to the mountains in your life right now, commanding them in Jesus' name to obey the authority you have been given:

2. When it comes to overcoming sin, Satan has no authority on the earth apart from what we as people give him. When we yield to Satan and his temptations, we give him authority to work through us. When we resist him, he has to flee (James 4:7).

What are a few areas where the enemy tries to take you down? What lies does he tell you and what is God's truth?

Chapter Highlights: (*No More No* pp. 215-216)

Read the Chapter Highlights and Application for review and inspiration.

Section 4—You Can Do It!

Read:

No More No pp. 217-222 (You Can Do It!)

Verse: (Pray it as you say it 10 times and make it your truth!)

"Everything is possible for him who believes."

Mark 9:23

1. As we finish this journey together, and you begin your own, never forget that everything truly is possible when you simply believe Jesus. Fix your eyes on His eyes of love, grab hold of His capable hands and step out on the water with Him. Even when you mess up or miss it at times, He will hold onto you tightly and pull you through every embarrassment, challenge or persecution.

   Life in Christ truly boils down to three things—faith, hope and love:

      a. **Faith:** Trust God. He is big and He will be big through you.

      b. **Hope:** Silence the lies of the enemy and dream with Jesus.

      c. **Love:** Allow His love to transform your life and your world.

2. Continue to build up your faith.

   List practical ideas to help you grow in confidence and keep stepping out of your GPS truck to deliver gifts from God's heart. (See p. 218 in *No More No* for ideas.)

Here are a few more ideas for growth:

Do a Treasure Hunt in Your Bible: I created a treasure hunt for myself to find all the places in the Bible where it talks about saying *yes* to God's promptings, laying down our lives for others and walking in radical love. I wrote "GPS" beside each passage and circled it. Now I can quickly flip through my Bible and find those encouragements for me or others.

Attend a *Be Jesus* Event or Invite us to Speak: Be Jesus events are held in various locations around the world. Participate in a *Be Jesus Conference* or event, or better yet, host one at your church. (You can watch videos on our site of past conferences, and then contact us if you would like to host a conference or have me (or others from our ministry) speak at your church, retreat, Bible study or other gathering.

Organize Outreaches: Your group may want to have a monthly outreach together to keep each other encouraged and to share the love of Jesus with people in your area. Or go on shopping trips and incorporate listening for God's voice into the outing.

Keep Recording Your Stories: If you continue to write down or audio/video-record your encounters with people, you will have something to cheer you on when the enemy tries to discourage you.

3. Please write me! I would love to hear how *No More No* and/or this study helped you grow. You would be amazed how little feedback authors get, so please email me at Contact@CrazyAboutYou.org. You can share both positives and negatives. I am always open for ideas for improvement!

You Can Do It! Just like riding a bike or driving a car, expressing God's heart will get easier and less scary the more you say *yes* and just do it. You and God make a great team. He creates the gifts and you deliver them, so trust your Boss, have fun and go for it!

Week 9: Group Wrap-Up

Group Session #10

- Will someone please open us in prayer?

- [Discuss any business.]

- Last week's "You Can Do It":
    - ❖ How did it go as you followed the promptings of the Holy Spirit?
    - ❖ When you didn't feel a prompting, did you remember to still ask people if they had prayer needs as you bumped into them throughout the week?
    - ❖ Did you remember to walk into every setting expecting God to work through you? If you did, what happened?

- "You Can Do It" for the rest of your life:
    - ❖ Now you get to live like Jesus and work for God's Parcel Service the rest of your life!
    - ❖ Remember not to walk in guilt when you don't say *yes* to God's promptings. Just silence the enemy and go for it the next time.

- Section 1 Discussion: Power Up Your Super Suit
    - ❖ Read Galatians 3:26-27.
    - ❖ What does it mean to be clothed in Christ?
    - ❖ As soon as you believe in Jesus as your Savior and Lord, inviting the Holy Spirit to baptize you in His love and power, you become a superhero and a Parcel Wonder because you are clothed in Christ. If it helps, picture yourself inside a Jesus costume every day, but this costume comes fully loaded, similar to the Iron Man suit!
    - ❖ Let's read and discuss 3 or 4 of your favorite scriptures from pp. 126-127 of this guide, talking about the power you have been given with your Super Suit, and what being clothed in Jesus and filled with the Holy Spirit equips you to do on the earth.

- Section 2 Discussion: Discover the Real You
    - ❖ Read 2 Corinthians 5:17.
    - ❖ What does this verse mean?

- ❖ Read Romans 8:1.
- ❖ Thanks to Jesus and all that He suffered, you have the privilege of becoming a new creation once you are in Christ—once you are in your Super Suit. It is vital, then, that you discover what a new creation looks like so that you can fulfill the purposes God has for you—the real you.
- ❖ Let's discuss the importance of knowing that you are free from condemnation and why condemnation can destroy your effectiveness in the Kingdom.
- ❖ Did you all have a clear understanding of the section quoted from Andrew Wommack on pages 206-209 in *No More No* where he explains why we are completely forgiven, holy and righteous in God's sight?
- ❖ Your soul and your mind are renewed and transformed daily, but your spirit is a new creation and sin free. Once you fully grasp this, then you are able to walk in confidence and enjoy the love of the Father for you. Why do you think this is true?
- ❖ Knowing that God loves you passionately is another key to discovering the real you. Why is that true?
- ❖ Many people struggle to believe God is perfect in love because they falsely blame Him for things that are actually a result of man's free will, effects of a fallen world or our lack of faith for the supernatural. Have you struggled in this area or been taught incorrectly?

Section 3 Discussion: Take Back Your Authority
- ❖ Read Psalm 115:16.
- ❖ What does this verse mean?
- ❖ Not knowing the authority God has given us on the earth is another reason for much of the suffering and pain mankind experiences needlessly. God has given us, "the children of men," authority, but ever since Adam and Eve, the enemy has been robbing us of our authority—by convincing us that we don't have any. Do you agree?
- ❖ Jesus' mission was to destroy the works of the devil and the lies that stripped us of our inheritance, rights and authority on the earth. What lies does the enemy tell you?
- ❖ Let's read and discuss 3 or 4 of the verses from pages 130-131 of this study guide that talk about the authority we have been given on the earth.

❖ You will have tribulations and trials on the earth (John 16:33) because you are daily dealing with people who have free will to choose love and be a blessing or to choose evil and cause harm (yourself included). But that doesn't negate the areas where you do have power and authority. You have power and authority over sickness, disease, demons, animals, bugs, plants, the weather and mountains! Do you agree?

❖ What are the mountains in your life that need to move? (Keep silencing the lies, doubts and fears of the enemy and command those mountains to move!)

❖ When it comes to temptation to sin, we need to understand that Satan has no power over us. He only operates through the power we give him when we say *no* to God and *yes* to him.

❖ What does James 4:7 say and what does it promise us?

- Section 4 Discussion: You Can Do It!
    Let's read out loud from pp. 217-218 in *No More No*, and then read the stories on pp. 218-222 if time. Then discuss the ideas on p. 133 of this study guide.

- You did it! Great job!

- [Play worship music.] Let's kneel or lay before the Lord (if you can) and take turns praying out loud as we surrender the rest of our lives to His will, choosing to no longer say *no* to God's promptings, but to trust God with our *yes*! If anyone needs ministry afterward, please let us know.

My God Encounters

My God Encounters

My God Encounters

__My God Encounters__

My God Encounters

My God Encounters

My God Encounters

My God Encounters

Conversation Starters

"But everyone who prophesies speaks to men for their strengthening, encouragement and comfort" (1 Corinthians 14:3).

If God highlights someone:

- God just highlighted you with His love. (Then express that love and how God sees that person walking in victory and love.)

- This may sound weird, but I'm a Christian and I believe God speaks, and I feel He wants you to know....

- When I saw you, God gave me a picture of.... (Explain the picture as God shows you the meaning.)

- I was just praying God would bless you and I sensed....

- I am a Christian and God speaks to my thoughts all the time, but I am trying to get better at listening for what He wants to say to others.

- Do you have pain in your (mention where you feel the pain is)? I am discovering Jesus has given us authority over sickness and disease, and I am learning to take risks and pray for people.

- Are you gifted [musically, artistically, athletically]? (Then share how God wants to use that gifting or is using that gifting.)

- You are a person of great [influence, sensitivity, compassion]. (Then share how God wants to use that gift or is using that gift.)

For those you interact with such as cashiers, salesmen at the door or on the phone, coworkers, classmates, etc.:

- I like to pray for people I interact with throughout the day. Do you have any prayer needs?

- I was just praying God would bless you. Do you have any specific prayer needs for you or your family?

- (You may sense something as you tune into God's voice for them, so feel free to use one of the conversation starters from the first section.)

If someone has a noticeable injury:

- Ouch! How did you hurt yourself? I am a Christian and I have seen God heal my body and other people's. (Share a story and build their faith and yours, telling how Jesus died for all sickness and disease.) May I pray for you?
- That must have hurt....
- I am a Christian and I have seen God heal....

After beginning a conversation and sharing your words of love or impressions from the Lord, keep the conversation going with:

- What is your spiritual background?
- Do you have a relationship with the Lord yet?
- Are you a Christian? (If you sense they are.)

Explain the Good News:

If they aren't a Christian or you aren't sure if they know what that means, briefly explain that the bottom line is inviting Jesus to forgive your sins so that God's Spirit can live inside you on the earth and you can live with Him for eternity in heaven. Sin can't live with our perfect God. (Keep this simple, amazing message simple!)

Pray with them if they are ready:

If you sense they believe in Jesus and are ready to let Him take over in the driver's seat of their life, don't be afraid to ask them if they would like to receive forgiveness and give their lives to Jesus right then. (I have prayed with people behind cash registers and while being waited on in restaurants, so don't let that stop you.) Have them repeat a simple prayer of forgiveness and surrender, and then ask the Holy Spirit to baptize the person in His power and love. (Make sure to get their contact information and follow up with them.)

If they don't want to pray right then, tell them how they can pray at home. There is no magic prayer. It is receiving forgiveness and letting God lead your life! It is turning from a life of doing things your way to doing things God's way.

Leader's Guide and Tips

Your main goal is to have fun as you help inspire yourself and your group to tune into God's voice and say *yes* to God's promptings!

Before the first meeting:

- Make sure you have one *No More No* book and one *No More No Study Guide* for each person coming. The books can be ordered at CrazyAboutYou.org or directly on Amazon.com. Let people know the total cost beforehand so that they can bring checks or cash for you. (Or have them order the books online themselves.)

- Items to bring to meetings: nametags, pens, Bible or Bible app, timer

- Video for first meeting: Make sure you have a way for the group to watch the online video "Why the No More No Study can Change Your Life and Your World" found at www.CrazyAboutYou.org. Your laptop or a laptop connected to a TV will work. Make sure to get the Wi-Fi password from the host home beforehand.

- Prep before the meeting: Read "Greetings from Julie" and the "Kick-off Meeting." Also read through the first week's lesson, making sure you understand how it will work each week. Familiarize yourself with the book and the study guide. Also read through all these tips.

At the meetings:

- **Eye contact** as you speak with people individually and as you lead the group is vital. Everyone in your group needs to have eye contact from you in equal measures so they feel equally important and cared for. Your warmth and caring will heal hearts and give people confidence. Love through your eyes.

- **Be a great listener** and affirm what people say. Make positive comments about people's comments whenever possible. But also be aware that you may have to gently move the conversation along if you have someone who talks more than they should. Stress to the group at the beginning that you want everyone to talk equally throughout the study. Make sure you don't talk too much as well. Work hard to draw people out and get them answering questions and giving ideas. That is the beauty of small groups!

- **Be vulnerable.** The best leader is the one who has nothing to hide and nothing to prove. Demonstrate humility and vulnerability to your group so that they, too, can be open and honest with their challenges and fears. Please don't feel you have to pretend to have it all together. That will do more harm than good. When a leader shares his or her challenges, it opens the door for everyone else to be honest and vulnerable, and then you are able to truly help one another.

Practical Tips for Group Wrap-Up:

- Encourage your group to do the "Going Deeper Version" each week, but don't make them feel badly if they are only doing the reading in the "Quick Version." Be excited for them!
- The "Group Wrap-Up" doesn't follow along closely with the 4 sections of homework each week. This was done in an effort to keep the discussion shorter to allow more time for ministry and for practicing hearing God's voice. Please encourage your group that it will probably be easiest to read along with you in the Wrap-Up rather than trying to follow along in the 4 sections of their homework.

Practical Tips for Practice in a Safe Place:

- You will have all levels of people who have never listened for God's voice for others to those who do it regularly, so make sure to be sensitive to those just trying for the first time. Encourage them to start out by listening for one word for someone such as "courageous, tenderhearted or tenacious" and then they can expand on that one word. Or have them ask God for a simple picture or Bible verse and then expand on that.
- Always, always remind the group each time they practice that these words should strengthen, encourage or comfort each other. Prophecy isn't for pointing out faults or sins, or for bringing correction. If they do sense a battle going on, have them prophesy the victory that God sees and do it in a way that doesn't expose the person.
- Get excited when someone misses a word because they took a risk!

Practical Tips for Outreaches:

- Keep the outreaches lighthearted! The goal is to make this a lifestyle, so show them how to have fun and be relaxed while being Jesus' hands, voice and feet.
- Review the Conversation Starters before going out.
- Remind them to start out in their comfort zone. They don't have to say anything until they are comfortable. They can watch and learn.
- Make sure there is time to share stories at the end of each outreach. Have the group share positive and seemingly negative experiences, learning from both and encouraging one another.
- Again, praise people when they seem to miss a prophetic word. Remind them it is normal to grow in hearing God's voice. Paul knew we would sometimes make mistakes in discerning God's thoughts from our thoughts which was why he said to test words of prophecy (1 Thessalonians 5:20-21).